D0776972

What others are saying about
The New Edge in Knowledge

"Carla O'Dell and Cindy Hubert have written an amazingly down to earth, useful and practical book on knowledge management and its importance to modern business. Starting with the distinction between information and knowledge, they provide a viewpoint that leaves IT in the dust. Read it to prepare for tomorrow's world!"

—A. Gary Shilling, President, A. Gary Shilling & Co., Inc.

"A practical business approach to knowledge management, this book covers KM's value proposition for any organization, provides proven strategies and approaches to make it work, shares how to measure KM's impact, and illustrates high level knowledge sharing with wonderful case studies. Well done!"

—Jane Dysart, Conference Chair, KMWorld,
and Partner, Dysart & Jones Associates

"This book is a tour de force in the field of knowledge management. Read every single page and learn about best practices from the leading firms around the world. All of this and more from the company that leads the way in the field: APQC. I highly recommend it for your bookshelf."

—Dr. Nick Bontis, Director, Institute for Intellectual Capital Research

"Food for thought from two of the pioneers. Carla O'Dell and Cindy Hubert have been in the trenches with many of the organizations that have succeeded in leveraging KM for business benefit. They recognized early the symbiotic relationship between knowledge flow and work flow and have guided practitioners in the quest to optimize and streamline both."

—Reid Smith, Enterprise Content Management Director,
Marathon Oil Company

"Carla O'Dell and Cindy Hubert take knowledge management from vague idea to strategic enabler. In so doing, they clear up not only the whats, but the whys and the hows. This book establishes knowledge management as an organizational discipline. The authors offer a straightforward set of execution steps, coaching readers on how to launch their own knowledge management programs in a deliberate and rigorous way."

—Jill Dyché, Partner and Co-Founder, Baseline Consulting;
Author of *Customer Data Integration:*
Reaching a Single Version of the Truth

"The authors and APQC have put together an excellent 'how to' manual for Knowledge Management (KM) that can benefit any organization, from those experienced in KM to those just starting. The authors have taken their years of experience and excellence in this field and written a masterful introduction and design manual that incorporates industry best-practices and alerts readers to the pitfalls they are likely to encounter. This book needs to be in the hands of every KM professional and corporate senior leader."

—Ralph Soule, a member of the U.S. Navy

The New Edge in Knowledge

HOW KNOWLEDGE MANAGEMENT IS CHANGING THE WAY WE DO BUSINESS

Carla O'Dell

Cindy Hubert

APQC

WILEY

John Wiley & Sons, Inc.

Published by John Wiley & Sons, Inc., Hoboken, New Jersey.
Published simultaneously in Canada.

For general information on our other products and services or for technical support, please contact our Customer Care Department within the United States at (800) 762-2974, outside the United States at (317) 572-3993 or fax (317) 572-4002.

Wiley also publishes its books in a variety of electronic formats. Some content that appears in print may not be available in electronic books. For more information about Wiley products, visit our Web site at www.wiley.com.

Library of Congress Cataloging-in-Publication Data:
O'Dell, Carla S.
   The new edge in knowledge : how knowledge management is changing the way we do business / Carla O'Dell, Cindy Hubert.
       p. cm.
   Includes bibliographical references and index.
   ISBN 978-0-470-91739-8 (hardback); ISBN 978-1-118-01516-2 (ebk);
ISBN 978-1-118-01517-9 (ebk); ISBN 978-1-118-01518-6, (ebk)
   1. Knowledge management.   2. Organizational learning.   3. Information resources management.   4. Organizational effectiveness.
   I. Hubert, Cindy.   II. Title.
       HD30.2.O34 2011
       658.4'038–dc22

                                                                    2010045245

Printed in the United States of America

*To our husbands, families, and APQC family
for going the distance with us every time.*

Contents

Foreword

I first ran into Carla O'Dell in the mid-1990s at a remarkable conference held at the University of California at Berkeley. The conference was to celebrate the first appointment of a Xerox Distinguished Professorship in Knowledge and to honor the first holder of that chair, Ikujiro Nonaka. There were about 30 participants, academics, and practitioners, who were all pioneers in this burgeoning movement to better understand how knowledge works in organizations.

Almost all of those participants are still involved in this invisible college of knowledge researchers, and some of the leading actors in this ongoing drama remain Carla O'Dell and her colleagues at the American Productivity and Quality Center (APQC). Let's look at some of the main principles focused on knowledge management back in those beginning days.

- Knowledge is a fixed pool, a collection of resources that can be measured and used by standard management techniques.
- Technology is the key tool to unlock the value of this resource. The more technology, the better.
- Individuals are the critical unit of analysis in working with knowledge—the more productive the individual, the more knowledge is being used.

It is now clear in hindsight that these principles were developed with information in mind, not knowledge, and that they were not at all suitable to working with such an elusive intangible. It is because of these ideas that many knowledge management efforts ran into problems and that the whole subject began to fade in the minds of busy executives.

However, it didn't die out at all. In fact, it was undergoing a resurgence as I was writing this in 2010. And one of the reasons is the outstanding research and communication of that research by APQC. Their work is grounded, is focused on the actual experience of workers and managers trying to work with knowledge, and conveys findings in clear and easily absorbable forms. Their yearly conference is one of the best places on Earth to learn what is happening in the field—direct from those rare birds, the reflective practitioners.

Based on this work and other efforts around the world, we now know quite different things about working with knowledge (in contrast to information).

- Knowledge is better understood as a flow. It is highly dynamic, nonlinear, and difficult to measure or even to manage. Working with it entails new techniques that we are still learning about.
- Although technology surely has its place, working with knowledge is primarily a human activity needing human organization and understanding.
- Knowledge in organizations is profoundly social and best managed in groups, networks, communities, and practices.

I can go on about all we have learned in the days since that Berkeley conference. But perhaps it is enough to stop here and salute Carla and her esteemed coworkers at APQC, who have steadfastly carried forth the mission of understanding knowledge as the critical thing that it is for organizational as well as human progress.

—Larry Prusak, founder and executive director
of the Institute for Knowledge Management

Preface

Knowledge management has come of age, and it is now time to reap the benefits. Organizations that figured out how to secure meaningful value from helping people share knowledge are thrilled with their results and can't imagine working any other way. How else would their far-flung teams collaborate? How else would content and knowledge be shared just in time, with just enough detail, and just for the employee or team seeking it? Some organizations have built their entire business models around their capability to manage and share knowledge. They can't compete without it.

This book tells you how leading organizations achieve great results in knowledge management, or KM, and provides the strategic principles to help you do the same in your organization. Nonprofit research firm APQC has almost 20 years of hands-on experience in KM benchmarking, best practices, and implementation with the best organizations in the world. This book shares what we have learned while leading APQC's efforts and directs you to even more tools and resources.

KM's New Playing Field

Many recent changes in the way we do business and communicate in general have exciting implications for KM. Even companies and governments with mature KM programs have adjusted their strategy for these game-changing trends.

- The digital world has begun to reshape KM. Online social networking has shaken up traditional KM. Although new technologies always present new challenges, no KM function can ignore this opportunity. Enterprise 2.0 tools may be the best thing to happen to KM since the water cooler.
- In their personal lives and on the job, employees have become digitally immersed. Employees of all ages expect more

engagement and access to information and want work processes that reflect the ease with which they communicate outside of work.

- Smart phones and other mobile devices now allow us to communicate and share any place, any time, and with anyone. KM can take advantage of these always-on and always-on-you devices to make content available to employees at their most *teachable moment.*
- A huge demographic is now leaving the work force. As baby boomers exit the playing field, their absence puts a greater need on incoming employees to get up to speed quickly.

These societal shifts have changed the power dynamics for how all organizations operate. An increasingly savvy workforce is dictating how and when they need information, and organizations face tremendous opportunities to turn individual employees' knowledge into organizational intellectual assets.

Employees need vivid, relevant examples and practical advice for everyday work. Executives need a tangible and substantial return on investment. And organizations need to respond to the forces at work and create new approaches. In this new environment, KM is an absolutely necessary core business practice to face the competition. With it, employers can reasonably expect better knowledge-based decisions from their workforce.

Making the Right Game Plan

This book addresses the core strategic issues in making KM successful. We're not just throwing around the term *strategic;* let us emphatically state: This book provides a strategic road map for an enterprise KM program. We share APQC's vast body of knowledge from hundreds of research and advisory efforts. In addition to providing practical and proven advice, we help you build a business case using examples from Accenture, ConocoPhillips, Fluor, IBM Global Business Services, MITRE, Petrobras, Schlumberger, the U.S. Department of State, and many others we have been privileged to work with.

Chapter 1, "Positioning Knowledge Management for the Future," provides the foundation for our discussion of key strategic concerns in KM, as well as detailing KM program objectives and new forces in the KM arena. It also introduces a framework to guide your enterprise KM program design efforts.

Chapter 2, "A Call to Action," details how to identify and focus attention on the value proposition and critical knowledge and then provide tools to map and understand that knowledge.

Chapter 3, "Knowledge Management Strategy and Business Case," focuses on the KM program strategy. We show you how to build the business case for enterprise KM to address strategic objectives. We also review how critical knowledge must flow and how a KM program matures.

Chapter 4, "Selecting and Designing Knowledge Management Approaches," describes the primary categories of KM approaches and provides tools, questions, design principles, and key concerns in selecting the right portfolio of approaches. We also explain how to incorporate these approaches into employees' work flow.

Chapter 5, "Proven Knowledge Management Approaches," examines the characteristics, benefits, challenges, and critical success factors for implementing proven approaches such as communities of practice.

Chapter 6, "Emerging Knowledge Management Approaches," examines the promise of Web 2.0 tools and details KM approaches such as wikis, microblogs, social bookmarking, and tagging. We also address best-practice characteristics, measurement tools, and unique challenges posed by these new opportunities.

Chapter 7, "Working Social Networking," further dives into Web 2.0 tools by focusing on the potential of enterprise social networking and provides cautions and guidelines for harnessing the exciting possibilities for KM, including an in-depth discussion of expertise location.

Chapter 8, "Governance, Roles, and Funding," lays out the people infrastructure for an enterprise KM program. We examine strategic concerns surrounding your KM program governance model, core roles, staffing numbers, and funding concerns.

Chapter 9, "Building a Knowledge-Sharing Culture," focuses on the all-important people issues and executive involvement. It provides branding and collaboration advice, a communication strategy template, communication plan discussion points, recognition approaches, and advice for engaging employees.

Chapter 10, "Measuring the Impact of Knowledge Management," explains how to address common measurement needs with measures by KM program maturity level, a measurement model and alignment worksheet, analytics, and a reporting structure.

Chapter 11, "Make Best Practices Your Practices," explains how to keep a strategic focus for your KM program as change management and implementation demands evolve. Bringing together the guiding principles we detail throughout the book, we focus on how to ensure your KM program continues to mature and improve.

The Appendix, "Case Studies," chronicles four leading organizations with outstanding enterprise KM programs.

Each chapter details the pertinent strategic concerns and then directs you to key implementation resources available online at www.newedgeinknowledge.com.

Who Should Step Up to the Plate?

Whether you are just starting with KM, starting over, or trying to figure out the next big thing, this book could save you a lot of time and money. We tackle the pressing issues in KM today, keeping in mind the enduring principles and the emerging opportunities to successfully manage knowledge.

The perspectives and robust methodologies in this book can help those just getting started as well as those committed to taking their KM programs to world-class levels.

- Many executives are dismayed by the amount of money they spend on KM technology. Information moves around, but what happens to knowledge? Are people smarter? Making better decisions? Selling more? Connecting the dots? Not without a KM strategy that works. This book can help executives spend KM dollars more wisely and understand their role in creating an organization that thrives on its knowledge.
- KM champions and professionals charged with designing and implementing KM programs want help getting funding, getting started, and getting results. This book can help these practitioners create a solid business case for enterprise KM, as well as engage participants. Most importantly, our book provides a practical and strategic approach to translate individual knowledge into action.

This book is not a guide for implementing communities of practice or localized efforts. With APQC, we have written such guides and have 28 best practices reports, numerous books, and more than 100 detailed case studies of organizations with best practices in KM. Instead, this book is a strategic road map. Many organizations have inefficient and disparate local efforts to manage knowledge; others have repeatedly made unsuccessful organization-wide KM efforts, wasting precious funding and goodwill. And still, some organizations are just starting to try to initiate KM efforts. This book addresses how all such organizations can implement an organization-wide KM strategy that works. The end result is a robust and steadfast enterprise KM program.

Keep in mind that KM has had its ups and downs. At various times, pundits have declared KM dead or a failure. A lot of IT vendors went belly-up in the dot-com bust. They hyped their tools as synonymous with KM, which, of course, they weren't. But organizations still need to get information and knowledge from the employees who have it to those who need it. Those needs never went away. Those needs continue to grow as organizations become more global.

APQC never stopped working in KM. Our research and practice is booming, and our members achieve great results and build deep competency. Our goal is to help everyone, including you, operate at the highest level of KM maturity and results.

Acknowledgments

We thank APQC and our colleagues, families, and friends for allowing us the time to write. Quiet time for dialogue and deep reflection are hard to come by. With their help, writing this book afforded us that.

The best ideas in this book came through collaboration, and we had fun working with each other. We would have nothing to write about without our APQC members and customers and the best-practices organizations we have studied and worked with. You will meet some of them in this book. We treasure the relationships and the shared learning we have with each of them. And we extend a special thanks to the members of our KM Advanced Working Group, who keep us on the cutting edge of KM:

- Baker Hughes Inc.
- IBM Global Business Services
- Marathon Oil Corporation
- Petrobras
- Research in Motion Ltd.
- SAP
- Singapore Armed Forces
- State Farm Mutual Automobile Insurance Company
- U.S. Navy Carrier Team One
- U.S. Army Armament Research, Development, and Engineering Center (ARDEC)

And we thank representatives from the four primary organizations featured in the book for their generosity in sharing their KM experiences over the years with us and with hundreds of APQC members through site visits and case studies. These representatives include: Dan Ranta, Yvonne Myles, and their marvelous teammates at ConocoPhillips; John McQuary, Tara Keithley, and their stellar team at Fluor; Bryant Clevenger, Ruth McLenaghan, and Isabel

Dewey leading the way in IBM Global Business Services; and Jean Tatalias and Marcie Zaharee, who make sure MITRE knows what (and who) it knows.

Without the masterful hand of our APQC editor and project manager, Paige Leavitt, this book could have been just a set of models, reflections, and anecdotes rather than an attempt to transfer our knowledge. We can't thank her enough.

And we give a special thanks to members of our APQC KM team: David Bullinger, Chris Gardner, Jim Lee, Darcy Lemons, Janis Mecklenburg, Lauren Trees, Jeff Varney, Erin Williams, and Angelica Wurth. They make us and our customers all look good.

1

Positioning Knowledge Management for the Future

In 2000, Brad Anderson, then president of electronics retailer Best Buy, called the American Productivity and Quality Center (APQC) for help. Wal-Mart, Target, and other discount retailers were hotly pursuing Best Buy's customers. Anderson wanted Best Buy to exploit the knowledge gained from its head start selling digital electronics. If selling electronics became solely a commodity business, then Best Buy might not win. But Brad knew that Best Buy's customers were struggling to keep up with the explosion of digital technology and would value knowledgeable guidance from the company's sales employees. Brad had just read our book *If Only We Knew What We Know* (Grayson and O'Dell 1998) and called APQC to see if knowledge management (KM) could help.

Fast forward to 2010: Best Buy has grown from 400 to 1,400 stores in the United States and Canada, with another 2,600 stores around the world, and from $6 billion to $50 billion in annual sales (*DailyFinance* 2010). More impressively, Best Buy continues to outperform its competitors in revenues and margins.

Of course, KM is only a part of the reason; but if you ask the folks at Best Buy, they will tell you the ability to share what they know and act on it has been a large part of their success. The early communities of practice that started in 2000 to share knowledge across the stores set the stage for the matrix of knowledge-sharing approaches the organization has today.

Everyone competes on how much they know. Companies lose sales, governments lose battles (especially with terrorists), and people lose jobs when they don't have the strategy and means to connect the dots. But there's a clear solution.

Although you can't manage the knowledge in people's heads, you *can* capture, enable, and transfer knowledge and best practices.

What Is Knowledge Management?

From a practical perspective, we define *knowledge* as information in action. Until people take information and use it, it isn't knowledge. In a business context, knowledge is what employees know about their customers, one another, products, processes, mistakes, and successes, whether that knowledge is tacit or explicit.

APQC defines *knowledge management* as a systematic effort to enable information and knowledge to grow, flow, and create value. The discipline is about creating and managing the processes to get the right knowledge to the right people at the right time and help people share and act on information in order to improve organizational performance.

Organizations implement a *KM program* to institutionalize and promote knowledge-sharing practices. An enterprise KM program is usually a centralized, organization-wide effort to standardize and excel in KM. Enterprise does not have to be the entire corporation. *Enterprise* may refer to a business entity that is a meaningful cost or revenue center performing work supporting a defined region of customers. Examples include divisions such as IBM Global Business Services and government agencies such as the Department of State or the U.S. Navy. Within such a program, organizations implement KM *approaches* such as communities of practice, expertise location systems, and wikis to formalize and enable knowledge sharing. KM *activities,* on the other hand, are all of the things KM professionals do to support the program and its approaches, such as planning and design, change management, communication, training, and budgeting. Through these activities and approaches, KM programs should:

- Connect employees to one another to help them excel at their jobs
- Connect employees to knowledge assets (just enough, just in time, and just for them)

- Connect those with experience or know-how with those who need it

These actions will accelerate the rate of learning; cut down the risks of not knowing and repeating mistakes; and retain knowledge assets when people move, leave, or retire.

This all requires strategy. To enable KM to succeed in your organization, you will need a well-thought-out strategy. You can waste a lot of money, time, and goodwill by implementing KM approaches before you've determined how your organization will overcome silos, knowledge hoarding, and "not invented here" resistance. You can waste even more of your organization's resources by simply adopting an information technology (IT) tool and calling it a KM program. (Technology alone will not ensure engagement and value.) Let us help you position KM in the sweet spot of knowledge and business strategy. We know what works.

Explicit and Tacit Knowledge

Explicit knowledge (also known as *formal* or *codified* knowledge) comes in the form of documents, formulas, contracts, process diagrams, manuals, and so on. Explicit knowledge may not be useful without the context provided by experience.

Tacit knowledge (also known as *informal* or *uncodified* knowledge), by contrast, is what you know or believe from experience. It can be found in interactions with employees and customers. Tacit knowledge is hard to catalog, highly experiential, difficult to document, and ephemeral. It is also the basis for judgment and informed action.

KM in a New Context

One of us—Carla—wrote her first book on how to implement KM, *If Only We Knew What We Know*, in 1998, when the discipline was less than a decade old (Grayson and O'Dell).

What a difference a decade makes. Witness September 11th, the Iraq and Afghanistan wars, the rise of China as a superpower, global warming, the near meltdown of the global financial system in 2008 and 2009, and the Gulf of Mexico oil rig explosion and resulting pollution in 2010.

The changes are just as substantial as we edge closer to the realm of KM: rising Internet and broadband access, the explosion of mobile devices and smartphones, the continued rise in virtual work and global teams, the international equalization of competitive prowess and knowledge,[1] the decline of readership for the printed word, the rise of digital readership, and on and on.

It would be hard to overstate how profoundly these developments have both challenged and enhanced the promise and practice of KM. KM's core objectives haven't changed, but how we accomplish them has. In this section, we zoom in on the forces affecting organizations and KM now and for years to come. We offer advice throughout this book to deal with them.

A Ready User Base

More than 1.8 billion people have access to the Internet (Shirky 2010). As of July 2010, there were more than 500 million Facebook users (Gaudin 2010) with more than 55 million updates a day and 3.5 billion content pieces shared weekly (Giles 2010). With 4 billion mobile phones in use (CIA 2009b), Neilsen expects smartphones to outnumber cell phones by 2011 (Entner 2010).

Force 1: Digital Immersion

We are experiencing the incursion of the Internet and digital technology into almost every aspect of our lives. Wireless connections and mobile devices have made the Internet available from almost anywhere, and ever-increasing bandwidth has enabled the rise of streaming video and other high-impact content. Employees of all ages spend 70, 80, or even 90-plus hours a week in front of laptops and smartphones, conducting a mix of professional and personal business. Expectations of 24/7 connectivity are affecting the way we work and live.

Many people are comforted by the feeling that they're always getting things done—responding to e-mails in meetings, taking calls in line at the supermarket, and so on. But that feeling may be an illusion.

Are today's employees as savvy as they appear at multitasking? Not according to Clifford Nass, a professor at Stanford University and the director of the Communication Between Humans and Interactive Media Lab. His data suggest that even the brightest people are hampered by an unwillingness (or inability) to focus on one thing at a time. Nass and his research team predicted that multitaskers might be good at three things:

1. *Filtering.* Focusing on what's relevant while ignoring distractions and extraneous information.
2. *Switching.* Moving between tasks quickly and getting up to speed with a minimum amount of ramp-up time.
3. *Organizing their memories.* Transferring information from short-term to long-term memory to ensure that important facts are retained.

But his research results then indicated the opposite: "It turns out multitaskers are terrible at every aspect of multitasking," Nass writes. "They're terrible at ignoring irrelevant information; they're terrible at keeping information in their head nicely and neatly organized; and they're terrible at switching from one task to another" (2010).

Even more disturbing, almost all the research participants *thought* they were good at these aspects of multitasking.

If you are familiar with Lean manufacturing techniques, you know that set-up time does not add value. And when you switch what you are working on, there is set-up time. HP research indicates it can take 15 minutes to fully reset your focus after an interruption (Friedlander 2010). You are not actually multitasking. Instead, you toggle between tasks and lose start-up time every time you switch back. And there is a good possibility that you will forget something before you get back to it.

The findings are clear: While supposedly getting more done in less time through our immersion in digital technology, we are actually working more slowly, absorbing information less effectively, and hampering our capacity for analytic reasoning.

A study by the University of California at Irvine found that the average professional switches between work activities every three minutes and five seconds (Pattison 2008). A similar study involving Microsoft employees reinforced that when employees were interrupted by e-mail or instant messages, it took them an average of 15 minutes to return to more complex mental tasks like computer programming or writing reports. This kind of multitasking decreases productivity while increasing stress and feelings of overload. "When people are switching contexts every [few] minutes, they can't possibly be thinking deeply," writes Professor Gloria Mark of the University of California at Irvine (Lohr 2007).

If we don't have any choice and we're going to hire (and even encourage) multitaskers, then what kind of KM scaffolding are we going to need to create to get thoughtful work done? We must adapt content and messages to align with employees' time and attention limitations. For KM, the implications are that:

- We should assume employees are multitasking.
- It isn't making them perform better or pay attention to every-thing they see.
- We shouldn't design KM approaches that interrupt employees any more than they already are.
- Even if a piece of information or knowledge is critical to retain, we can't assume employees will remember it when they need it. It has to be there at the *teachable moment*.

Force 2: Social Computing

Nearly one-fourth of the world's more than 1.8 billion Internet users have profiles on social networking sites such as Facebook, LinkedIn, and MySpace (Miniwatts 2009). And 75 million are signed up on Twitter (Gaudin 2010). LinkedIn, the networking site for profession-als, has more than 70 million users (Rao 2010). Facebook alone will likely exceed 600 million users by 2011. To put this number into perspective, if Facebook were a country, it would be the third most populous after India and China (Giles 2010). Even more staggering, in just one month, Facebook users post more than 3.5 billion pieces of content.

With that much practice, it's no surprise that employees feel at ease with social networking tools. Social computing, Web 2.0, and the rise of social media are transforming KM. It is so good for KM that if we didn't have it, then we would have to invent it.

We define *social media* as Internet technology that allows people to generate content and interact in a way that creates new information and value. Social media becomes *social computing* when applied to a noncommercial intent among people to share and co-create. *Web 2.0* tools are specific social computing technologies that are relatively easy to adopt and master. From these developments come *Enterprise 2.0* applications, which tailor social media for business by addressing privacy concerns and helping to align a wealth of internal knowledge and information sources within organizations and thus enable social computing.

A defining feature of social computing is the reliance on the employee—not the organization—to create, share, rate, and consume content. Simply by having the means to do so, each employee can be an author, arbiter, and consumer at once.

A second defining feature of social computing is that the content improves the more people interact with and build on it. Wikis and open innovation sites work best when informed people contribute; ratings are arguably better and more accurate the more people contribute; metatags are more useful the more they are applied; folksonomies can rival corporate taxonomies when many people tag and rate content; and good sites and documents rise to the top of search requests the more often people bookmark them and share those bookmarks.

We believe social computing tools are reinvigorating KM by making it easier for employees to participate in knowledge creation while showing them the value of sharing with an online network of peers. By borrowing ideas from Facebook, organizations have been able to help employees connect across disparate regions. Similarly, sites like Wikipedia have popularized ways to collaborate and co-author content. Since a majority of employees are already familiar with the features and have seen their value, it is easier to build buy-in and may be easier to drive participation.

Many organizations—especially those in government and in highly regulated industries—continue to be extremely concerned with the ramifications of these barrier-crushing applications. For example, standards around trust are relaxing when it comes to the democratization of information and opinion. And social computing is altering the determination of who are experts. But the most pressing concerns surround security and privacy: what stays behind the firewall and what employees actually share with one another and the world at large. KM professionals must find ways to capitalize on the positive aspects of these new technologies while addressing these concerns.

Another key concern is how employees participate. Social computing works when enough people participate. And participation has historically has been the biggest challenge for KM. We see an important, sobering parallel in content contribution:

- On Facebook, 80 percent of the content is posted by 20 percent of users.
- Only one in five Twitter account holders have ever posted anything, and 90 percent of content is posted by 10 percent of the users (Moore 2010).

Keep those statistics in mind when thinking about participation rates for KM approaches using Web 2.0 tools inside your organization. A small percentage of people are the core contributors of content. Even popular social computing approaches require KM professionals to marshal an effective KM strategy and infrastructure to elicit engagement.

Changing Expectations

The Economist reports: "As people become increasingly used to sharing and collaborating outside the workplace, they are coming to expect firms to be more open and collaborative places too. . . . Doing business, after all, boils down to managing a complex web of relationships with customers, suppliers, and others" (2010).

Force 3: Demographics and Dynamics

We could get so caught up in the hype around generational differences at work (which may not be that great) that we may be overlooking the elephant in the room: retirement of the huge baby boomer generation. Many organizations face looming knowledge retention and transfer issues, regardless of industry, annual revenue, or their number of employees.

The retirement of a record 77 million baby boomers has the potential to result in huge losses of critical tacit knowledge, including the loss of organizational and technical knowledge on key processes and competencies. And churn from reorganizations, rapid growth, layoffs, internal redeployments, and new business models for offshoring work require just as much careful identification and transfer of knowledge. We've also seen skilled employee shortfalls in key disciplines and time-to-competency issues for those entering the workforce. Employees—especially new hires—face steeper, longer learning curves at the same time that employers are looking for faster revenue and higher productivity.

The scarcity of talent will be a driving force in KM. "Fewer younger people will be working to support a significantly larger older generation in the future," PricewaterhouseCoopers writes. "Millennials will be a powerful generation of workers" (2007).

Despite the handwringing every generation expresses about the next one, since the beginning of the Industrial Revolution every generation has been more productive than the previous one. Innovative technologies along with education and free market models have been the reason. Organizations will also benefit from incoming generations' increased desire to share knowledge (PricewaterhouseCoopers 2007).

KM needs to adapt to these evolving demographics and power dynamics. We're just seeing the first wave of a much larger phenomenon. Employees increasingly expect more engagement and information and want to achieve it in the same way they do in their personal lives.

We have one final point about the much-ballyhooed generational differences. Although some differences do exist, some of the behaviors we interpret as generational differences are actually "stage of life" differences. Twenty-something workers have always had different interests and priorities than their fifty-something colleagues.

Force 4: Mobile Devices and Video

The tagline "There's an app for that" has entered our lexicon, and everyone seems to be perpetually in a "Crackberry" prayer mode or immersed in their iPhone to the exclusion of all else. So what? Smartphones have been around for a relatively long time. There are well-established company policies and precedents for how to manage security; who pays for the device and its text, voice, and data charges; how to ensure the security of information; and how the IT organization can establish, manage, and integrate the whole system.

What are not well established are guidelines for KM professionals to capitalize on this ubiquitous, addictive pocket computer. What is appropriate to share through that tiny screen? How much do employees want to know, and when do they want to know it? What can we learn from RSS, alert systems, and Twitter to communicate with employees?

We also believe the future belongs to streaming video, and KM will benefit. Too expensive until now, cheap digital video is now literally in the hands of millions of people. YouTube and big bandwidth have made video a feasible and desirable medium for millions of average people to teach, learn, and share.

Demands to "show me, don't tell me" make video far superior to text for communicating something physical (for example, how to open a banana like a monkey). It is also terrific for communicating emotion. Now the buzz is to use it for a wide range of internal communication and not just the annual CEO speech.

Yet many, if not most organizations block access to YouTube. It's a quixotic effort, considering the sophistication of the personal devices employees have at their disposal. Organizations—and KM programs—would benefit by instead taking advantage of employees' comfort and familiarity with mobile devices and streaming video. In time, more powerful enterprise applications will be developed for mobile devices and streaming video, which will expand the power of these tools for finding and sharing information.

Is Your KM Program Ready?

The Economist predicts that more than 600 million people will use their phones to tap in to social networks by 2013 (Giles 2010). KM needs to be able to say, "We have an app for that."

These are some of the major forces at work on KM today. We maintain that KM can help the digitally induced, shrinking-attention-span, socially networked, information overloaded, smartphone-obsessed, and busy knowledge worker of today.

Primary Directives

This leads us to two major directives for any KM program.

Have KM Ready at the Teachable Moment

The term *teachable moment* refers to a time when an individual is most receptive to learning something (*Encarta* 2009). It involves the idea that the thing learned at that moment, when the individual is faced with a problem or an opportunity, is more likely to be used and retained than if it comes at another time. Think of teachable moments as windows of opportunity to provide knowledge assets to an employee when they are needed and the employee is most receptive.[2] Better decisions and more productive actions result.

KM was born to address the teachable moment.

KM programs can take advantage of emerging technologies and design innovative ways to enable knowledge sharing at these teachable moments, with just enough detail, just in time, and just for that employee.

The nature of teachable moments, however, makes this a challenge. They are somewhat unpredictable and can be fleeting. If employees can't get an answer to a question when they need it, then they may not ask again. Or they will go with the first answer they find, which may not be the best one. And although sometimes we can orchestrate a teachable moment, this isn't always the case. In addition, organizations operate more virtually than they have in the past, which reduces the face-to-face opportunities that are such a rich environment for creating and responding to teachable moments.

Manage Knowledge Above and In the Flow of Work

We stumbled across the idea of above and in the work flow with regard to KM in a 2007 post to the *Transparent Office* blog by Michael Idinopulos, referring to the difficulty of getting people to use wikis. We think it offers a useful framework for being conscious of the kind of KM program you design.

Enabling employees to do their work more easily—by collaborating and capturing and sharing knowledge without an additional burden or interruption on their part—is doing KM *in* the work flow. Asking employees to stop their work process to move to another mode to reflect, capture, or share is doing KM *above* the work flow.

Working above the flow isn't always bad. Even creating a KM strategy is above the work flow of the core lines of business. But working above the flow can be resource-intensive. And if you want employees to step out of their work to support the flow of knowledge, then you will need to explain why and ensure there is an intrinsic or extrinsic payoff.

The trick is to balance *above* and *in* the work flow. For example, responding to the teachable moment by definition is in the work flow, but it is still necessary to create the content or access to the content and people, which is an activity above the work flow. That takes resources and is money well spent.

The themes of the teachable moment and above versus in the work flow weave their way throughout the book to keep our awareness focused on the needs of employees and the implications of the KM programs we design.

Showcasing KM Leaders

Throughout this book, we use examples from many great KM programs. In addition, to provide you with a comprehensive look at KM programs in action, we frequently showcase four organizations with mature, organization-wide KM programs.

The first two, ConocoPhillips and Fluor Corporation, are exemplars of weaving knowledge sharing into the functional fabric and structure of their organizations through traditional KM communities of practice. No less impressive, IBM uses a more fluid KM model, built on a user-driven paradigm and a portfolio of Web 2.0–driven KM approaches. KM at MITRE has always focused on enabling self-service through content management and expertise location, which now includes a cutting-edge Web 2.0 toolkit.

We have studied and worked with these four organizations—and so many others—for many years and have an intimate sense of their journey. A brief overview follows of their KM strategies and approaches. (We include examples throughout the book and case studies in the Appendix.)

ConocoPhillips

ConocoPhillips is an international, integrated energy company and the third-largest oil and gas company in the United States. ConocoPhillips's KM vision is to become "a workplace where employees continuously deliver additional value through global collaboration and expertise sharing." Its KM program addresses:

- *Consistent operations and organizational improvement.* To drive standardization and promote functional excellence
- *Size and complexity.* To facilitate global functionality
- *Asset maturity.* To support buildup and renewal of operations, including strategic partnerships
- *Knowledge access.* To improve the global availability of knowledge
- *Demographics.* To ease the workforce renewal process
- *Competitive differentiation.* To create a sustainable advantage through knowledge access and reuse

In promoting organization-wide knowledge sharing, its KM program leverages its 120-plus communities of practice, communications and training, a semantic analysis approach, global awards, activities, success stories, and a focus on connecting employees.

The way in which ConocoPhillips has changed employee behavior and improved employees' attitude toward knowledge sharing has spurred the success of various knowledge-retention tactics, including success story collection, benchmarking, and best practices and lessons-learned repositories.

This global energy company was named as one of the 2009 North American Most Admired Knowledge Enterprises (MAKE) by Teleos in association with the KNOW Network. ConocoPhillips's systematic KM program has saved hundreds of millions of dollars and changed the organization's culture.

Fluor

Fluor is one of the world's largest publicly traded engineering, procurement, construction, maintenance, and project management organizations.

For more than 20 years, Fluor informally used KM strategies and techniques to enhance collaboration and leverage collective knowledge. In 1999, the organization implemented a formal KM program to promote a consistent KM strategy across the enterprise. The CEO's mandate was to "transform Fluor into the premier knowledge-based services company."

Fluor recognized the need to collaborate and share knowledge across business units and regional boundaries, especially when executing multiple-party projects with competitors. Also, Fluor needs to tap in to experts anywhere in the world. Consequently, Fluor tightly linked its KM strategy to its overall strategic goals.

Fluor leverages communities of practice and a central portal for project work. Fluor now has more than 40 communities covering all major functional groups and several support services. The communities are responsible for sharing knowledge globally, enabling work processes, and bringing new employees up to speed quickly. In total, Fluor's communities have more than 20,000 members, which accounts for nearly every employee who has a technical, engineering, or managerial position.

The organization also leverages an expertise locator system, mentoring and people development programs, online collaboration and document management spaces, and process improvement methodologies to capture and transfer critical knowledge.

Fluor credits its KM program with driving significant revenue growth, higher revenue per employee, and cost reductions. Fluor was also named as one of the 2009 North American Most Admired Knowledge Enterprises.

IBM Global Business Services

IBM provides business insight and IT solutions to clients around the world. The organization's five major lines of business are global business services, global technology services, systems and technology, software, and global financing. We focus in this book on some of the great examples from IBM Global Business Services (GBS).

KM was formally recognized in IBM in 1995 and at the time was technology-driven. A people- and process-based KM program soon followed. Now built into the infrastructure of all of its operations, IBM GBS's KM strategy focuses on four elements: expertise, content, collaboration, and learning. The organization also focuses on how these elements are leveraged by different social systems (that is, how knowledge is shared by employees as well as members of teams and communities). Its on-demand approaches involve expertise location, communities, and the facilitated transfer of best practices.

As examples of its KM successes, IBM GBS's topic-based forums have 17,000 authors a month, resulting in a cost avoidance of $6 million annually. Its expertise location system has more than 111,000 profiles, resulting in $5.5 million savings annually.

The organization's KM program has completely integrated Web 2.0 applications by building many programs that then become commercial tools for other organizations to adopt. IBM GBS has an open environment to experiment and foster a continuing influx of new KM tools and approaches among IBM's business units.

MITRE

The MITRE Corporation is a nonprofit organization that provides expertise in systems engineering, IT, operational concepts, and enterprise modernization to address the critical needs of its sponsors, including the U.S. Department of Defense, the Federal Aviation Administration, and the Internal Revenue Service.

A high-level objective for MITRE is to "set the standard for excellence in business operations." MITRE's KM program was initiated in 1997 to leverage its diverse skills base organization-wide. It also supports content management and Web 2.0 tools for connecting employees and managing knowledge assets for sharing and reuse. Its KM program works with business units in a corporate planning, strategy, and championship function to collaborate and share knowledge.

The KM program is not focused on a single work group, system, or initiative. Instead, the organization relies on a set of KM approaches that currently include:

- A corporate intranet and information management system
- An internal wiki for collecting knowledge about projects, customers, organizations, technology, and staff
- A Web-centric project Rolodex that promotes knowledge sharing, especially with regard to the organization's technical work program
- Blogs for self-publishing, disseminating knowledge, and sharing informal information
- A central knowledge repository for all project information
- An enterprise search system for the organization's more than 2.2 million URLs, a core expertise finder and e-mail list searcher, and a source for locating technical exchange meetings
- A social tagging and bookmarking tool
- A microblogging tool that mirrors Twitter to facilitate social networking and expertise location

- A social networking tool for intelligence community professionals that automatically collects information about participants and provides contact recommendations

With the introduction of social networking and expertise location tools, MITRE has seen a paradigm shift regarding the accessibility of information. MITRE has third-party verification that its social networks and technology networks have a positive impact on personal innovation and that the frequency with which these networks are used is not as important as who employees connect with.

Closing Comments

Designing an enterprise KM program can be a complex process. To help you conceptualize your enterprise KM program, APQC developed the program design framework in Figure 1.1.

First, you establish the KM call to action by determining the business value proposition and what knowledge is considered critical. This helps set the direction for your KM efforts and secures leadership buy-in to formally develop a KM strategy. Strategy development occurs when you ask for resources to help design the KM strategy. This requires a business case and budget. Next, you are ready to form teams to design and launch KM approaches using detailed project plans and budgets. Then, to sustain and evolve, you benefit from the experience with the early deployments and pilots.

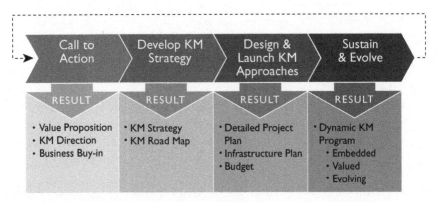

Figure 1.1   APQC's KM Program Framework and Road Map

You assess the capabilities you have, identify new opportunities, and develop an expansion strategy.

How long will all this take?

This may seem like a protracted journey, but the following chapters will show that it's not. In fact, we advocate 90-day cycles for each phase so you can get on with the business of showing value. (Taking too long to develop a KM strategy and program is a risk of a structured approach and a mistake.) Completing the first two can take only three months if you devote resources to it. You will come out of this cycle with an initial KM strategy with initial targets and budgets. Designing the initial approaches depends a bit on how complex and how many there are. But again, 90 days should be your stretch target to devise a plan and perhaps a pilot. Once the initial approaches are launched, 90-day cycles are appropriate for progress reviews and reporting on what you are learning and early indicators of engagement and impact.

Chapter 2 focuses on the call to action. Chapter 3 focuses on developing the strategy and business case. Chapters 4 through 7 help you determine the right KM approaches. Chapters 8 through 10 identify the infrastructure that will help you continually expand and improve as you evolve your KM program. Chapter 11 then wraps up everything you've learned into the guiding principles for your enterprise KM program, with the Appendix providing some in-depth examples of leading organizations.

Let's now dive in to how to establish an enterprise KM program that serves your organization's overall strategic goals.

Resources

The following APQC resources contextualize and expand on the topics discussed in this chapter:

- *If Only We Knew What We Know: The Transfer of Internal Knowledge and Best Practice*
- *Positioning KM for the Future*
- *Creating the Space for Critical Thinking and Decision Making*
- *Knowledge Sharing in a Web 2.0 World*
- *The Intersection of Innovation and Knowledge Management*
- *The Teachable Moment*

(Continued)

- Video: *The New Face(book) of Collaboration: Carla O'Dell at APQC's 2010 KM Conference*
- Video: *Five Ideal Future States for Knowledge Management: Carla O'Dell at APQC's 2009 KM Conference*

These resources—along with APQC's custom advisory services and more than 1,000 articles focused on KM—are available at www.apqc.org and through this book's Web site at www.newedgeinknowledge.com.

Notes

1. As discussed in Thomas Friedman, *The World Is Flat: A Brief History of the Twenty-First Century* (New York: Picador, 2007).
2. The concept of *sticky ideas* is related to the teachable moment concept. Sticky ideas are ones that are understood and remembered. See Chip Heath and Dan Heath, *Made to Stick: Why Some Ideas Survive and Others Die* (New York: Random House, 2007).

CHAPTER 2

A Call to Action

Buckman Laboratories International Inc., a specialty chemical organization, is one of the pioneers in KM. One of the keys to its long-term success is the clarity of its initial knowledge strategy. Buckman recognized that developing new products and putting product knowledge in the hands of its sales employees would make Buckman competitive with much larger players in its market. Therefore, the organization applied its limited KM resources to linking its sales and marketing functions with the knowledgeable people in its laboratories. The key KM measure of outcome was a percentage increase of new sales of products less than five years old. With this focused call to action, Buckman saw an increase of 50 percent of sales of new products. And due to the connections created to help knowledge flow between the sales people in the field and the experts in the laboratories, responses to customer inquiries about products now take hours instead of weeks.

As Buckman's story illustrates, a call to action is the spark to ignite your enterprise KM program. You've got to focus on knowledge that is valuable and durable enough to offer a sustainable, competitive advantage and justify the costs of retaining and transferring it. Building large repositories and content management systems to house all knowledge is a fruitless endeavor. The goal of managing knowledge is not to capture knowledge for its own sake. KM must serve your organization's strategic goals and the needs of employees using the knowledge.

This chapter explains how to create a call to action by identifying and prioritizing your organization's critical knowledge. This is how you will put your KM program on the right track. We explain how to identify critical knowledge and your organization's value proposition for helping knowledge flow, which will help set the direction for your KM strategy.

Knowledge Assets

A knowledge asset is tangible or intangible information or a link that is actionable. For example, a patent is a knowledge asset, but so is the relationship between the people in marketing and research and development (R&D) that enables the patent to be embedded in products.

Determine the Value Proposition

The first step in creating a call to action for KM is to understand the value proposition for enhancing the flow of critical knowledge. If you are newly appointed to develop a KM strategy, then what better place to start than to understand what is keeping executives up at night? If you have been leading KM for a while, then this is an opportunity to recalibrate and reconnect with executives around knowledge needs.

Who will do this? Your organization will need a KM leader. This person would lead the effort to determine your organization's knowledge needs and strategy. Sometimes called a *chief knowledge officer* or *director of KM,* your KM leader will structure and lead the enterprise KM program. They are usually highly competent, technically savvy, and experienced operations or IT experts. They are also typically well connected and know how to immediately pull together a small, but effective core group to develop the KM program. (We discuss the major KM roles in Chapter 8, but keep in mind that this key role will get the ball rolling.)

The KM leader should take a close look at your organization's strategic goals and talk to executives. Engaging these leaders can help pinpoint key challenges and opportunities that could benefit from improved knowledge flow.

The following five interview questions can help identify and focus attention (and resources) on the right problems and opportunities:

1. Does your current knowledge allow you to compete in the near term?
2. What knowledge will you need to help you innovate and meet long-term customer needs?
3. What market differentiator can be improved if knowledge and expertise is better shared and transferred?
4. Are there current and pending challenges or issues that are knowledge-related?
5. What will success look like?

The answers to these questions will help create a rationale for your enterprise KM program. It will also involve decision makers in your efforts and make them accountable for their input.

The first question helps you identify and prioritize the knowledge required to immediately improve performance. Look at your most urgent challenges or promising opportunities. Do you need to improve project schedule estimating? Do you need to compete on the speed of product innovation, as Buckman did? Or do you need to improve sales efficiency by reducing the time to close a sale?

We've seen challenges such as repeated customer complaints about a process that doesn't get fixed, making the same mistake across business units, loss of knowledge due to retirement, and a lack of access to experts by sales employees trying to make a complex sale. We've seen opportunities such as decreasing employees' time to competency by connecting new hires and experts and reducing the cost of innovation by embedding critical knowledge into product design processes.

The second question helps you understand threats and assumptions about knowledge in the context of your organization's long-term goals. If your organization is vulnerable to knowledge loss from retirement, redeployments, mergers, or downsizing, then you may need to identify expertise that will be leaving and develop approaches to capture and retain that core knowledge. Do you need to understand what skills or expertise exists inside your organization to meet specific organizational needs? How can a better flow of expertise improve the learning cycle for less experienced employees? Do you need to improve the time to competency for new hires?

For example, the identification of key competencies in tire design and other key disciplines helped Michelin target its call to action and drive the application of KM approaches to hasten the time to competency for new employees. (Universities don't teach tire design. Michelin has to train its own tire designers.)

The third question helps you focus on critical knowledge in your organization's value proposition to the marketplace. Do you want to compete on the basis of customer knowledge and service; product development and time to market; or low-cost, high-quality operations? Is your answer just one, two, or all three of these?

The fourth question helps you determine impending challenges that could stop your organization from meetings its strategic goals. The following criteria can help you assess what is most important to your organization. Does the challenge or opportunity:

- Align with your organization's strategies?
- Affect organizational performance?
- Demonstrate tangible value?
- Affect the retention of valuable knowledge?
- Leverage existing expertise to improve learning?

For example, Petrobras, a Brazilian-based energy company, forecasted a need for more than 100,000 new employees in the coming years. With a dramatic increase in new hires looming, Petrobras's call to action is to build sustainable knowledge and accelerate the learning curve on projects so that employees with less experience can manage complex projects in a shorter period of time. Consequently, Petrobras's KM goal is to decrease the time to competency for project managers from 10 down to 5 years by providing access to core organizational knowledge and transferring this knowledge and expertise through training, professional experience, and relationship networks.

Finally, the fifth question helps you understand what your leaders and stakeholders expect from your KM program. It will also help you manage their expectations by establishing the foundational requirements for your KM strategy.

For example, knowledge and its KM program are seen as strategic assets for ConocoPhillips. As part of its annual strategic planning and budgeting cycle, the director of KM at ConocoPhillips works with senior leaders to help define the knowledge strategy for each business unit. By envisioning how knowledge will help enable success, ConocoPhillips makes the flow of knowledge part of all employees' jobs.

In conclusion, the answers to these questions and the conversations around them will help identify your value proposition and start the conversation about what knowledge is critical to your organization and worth managing.

Involving Executives

The most compelling reason for senior managers to become involved in their KM programs is to ensure that all KM efforts relate to the overall strategy. Managing knowledge has to be embraced as offering a competitive advantage; otherwise, it is highly unlikely that it will become an organization-wide mode of operations.

Identify Critical Knowledge

Don't develop a KM strategy without thinking through what critical knowledge will serve your strategic goals. Trust us. Without it, you'll have employees getting on board a wagon with no horse to pull you through your journey.

Over the years, we've seen organizations develop great KM infrastructures, approaches, and activities with leading technologies. But when asked what knowledge they want to share and why, a well-meaning KM professional will say, "Oh, best practices to help us improve" or "Subject matter expertise, of course." But *what* best practices and *what* expertise?

You need a sharper focus. Building KM capabilities that connect employees and capture and share information is important, but being able to articulate specifically *what* knowledge needs those activities and approaches will address will lead to a clear call to action and more meaningful results. KM creates value only when it enables the creation and flow of the truly critical knowledge.

Fluor's executives speak of 2006 and 2007 as a perfect storm: Every sector was in a growth mode, requiring tremendous hiring globally. Hundreds of new employees were joining the organization every month, with a turnover rate of 25 percent in some locations such as New Delhi, India. Fluor had its value proposition and call to action.

In order to retain and transfer the right knowledge, Fluor set out to identify and prioritize which knowledge was most critical for it to retain and transfer so it could best deliver on its capital project commitments. The knowledge assets needed to continue to meet customer expectations and commitments were technical knowledge, regulatory knowledge, and work process–related knowledge. The technical knowledge refers to the complex processes used in the industries Fluor serves. Regulatory knowledge is based on the various industry and country codes applied around the world. The work process–related knowledge is for planning and executing complex projects. For Fluor, the resulting knowledge strategy was to create standardized methods and practices in technical, engineering, and regulatory knowledge domains so that work could be conducted anywhere in the world with the same high level of excellence.

Understanding the value proposition sets the stage for and directs a KM strategy. It focuses on what is happening in the work flow and what contributes to important organizational outcomes and results. Now, let's examine how to ensure that we can identify the critical knowledge so that it gets to the people who need it.

Just Enough, Just in Time, and Just for Me

How much knowledge is enough? Just make it simple for your employees. Think of KM practitioners as flight attendants who receive in-depth, detailed training on how to effectively evacuate an airplane. Think of your employees as the passengers who have at their fingertips only the information they need to move in the right direction. After all, your employees may not have much time to review the pertinent information before they need to act.

Locate Your Critical Knowledge

The wealth of knowledge within your organization is often hidden, sometimes because it resides in people and other times because it is buried in a folder. Obviously, before you can determine where critical knowledge should flow, you need to find out where it is and who has it. Knowledge maps provide a clear understanding of your knowledge assets and who has them. The tools in this section help identify in graphic form where critical knowledge resides.

Types of Knowledge Maps

A knowledge map acts as a snapshot in time to help your organization understand what knowledge it has and what it lacks (see Figure 2.1). The key is focusing on your organization's critical knowledge.

For different types of knowledge, different maps are appropriate. We have identified three main categories of knowledge maps, with seven different types of maps. To determine what type of map is most appropriate, select the focus that best serves your organization's call to action. (Visit www.newedgeinknowledge.com for templates of each type of map.)

1. Enterprise Knowledge Maps
   - *Strategic-level knowledge map.* Use this map to identify and gauge your organization's level of competency or expertise to meet its strategic goals. The gap analysis is critical: Once you've identified what you think is important, you should be able to create a plan of attack for closing gaps.

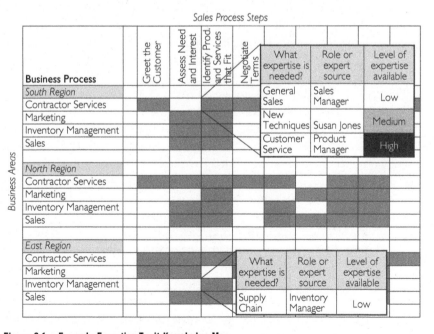

Figure 2.1   Example Expertise Tacit Knowledge Map

- *Expertise-level knowledge map.* Use this map to gain a broad understanding of what knowledge your organization has in various units, as well as to identify its risk of disappearing. This map also identifies strengths and opportunities in expertise, knowledge, and sharing behaviors, as well as key knowledge assets that need to be available to other parts of your organization. You can use this map in conjunction with HR succession planning maps to identify risk areas, plan for mitigation, and direct development plans for current employees.

2. Cross-Functional Knowledge Maps

- *Expertise tacit knowledge map.* Use this map to identify specific employees who are experts and their areas of expertise. This typically works best inside a business unit or a division with similar units. We have used this map most often to identify the right employees for after-action reviews and to highlight the appropriate employees to participate in a particular community of practice.
- *Technical/functional knowledge map.* Use this map to understand the strengths and gaps within specific technical or functional knowledge domains (e.g., ship design and component assembly). In conjunction with the competency/learning needs maps, this map can give senior managers a snapshot of expertise in critical technical disciplines and key competency areas.

3. Process-Explicit Knowledge Maps

- *Document-explicit knowledge map.* To create specific KM approaches, use this map to identify specific knowledge assets and content; knowledge needs; and the sources, recipients, locations, and formats of that knowledge.
- *Job- or role-based knowledge map.* Use this map to identify the knowledge needed for jobs or roles to perform specific processes. Although similar to the technical/functional knowledge map, this map adds a layer of specificity. This map helps create an inventory of the knowledge assets (and what format they are in) for each role, ultimately helping to identify gaps and strengths.
- *Competency/learning needs map.* Use this map to look more explicitly at learning or competency needs within various processes. Whereas the expertise overview knowledge map

ascertains current assets and the risks of losing those assets, this map examines the capabilities your organization needs to meet its strategic goals.

Knowledge Mapping Participants

Identify and recruit the appropriate roles to map knowledge.

1. A facilitator to set up and manage the exercise
2. A content editor to serve as the point person for collecting content and creating and distributing the knowledge map(s)
3. Subject matter experts to fill in gaps, authenticate results, and point to relevant sources of knowledge and competitive intelligence for any current repositories they manage
4. HR resources for expertise, competency, or learning assets
5. Appropriate managers to shape and scope the effort
6. Corporate librarians or data specialists as needed
7. Key process owners and operators

Steps to Map Knowledge

We caution you that there is no exact or perfect map for all situations. You will probably tweak any of these maps to suit your situation. Regardless of which type of map you require, there are 10 basic steps to follow:

1. Specify the process or focus area through which the critical knowledge flows. This is the scope of the map.
2. Specify the reason (i.e., the call to action) for mapping the knowledge.
3. Map the process or focus area.
4. Identify key decision points and cross-functional hand-offs.
5. Locate owners and stakeholders of highly valued activities.
6. Identify sources and recipients of critical knowledge.
7. Identify important knowledge assets needed for each step of the process.
8. Create an inventory of types of knowledge (explicit and tacit) used and needed.
9. Identify gaps, lack of connectivity, and information overload.

10. Develop a plan for reviewing, validating, and sharing the findings from your map.

We want to emphasize the importance in Step 9 of performing a gap analysis between what you found during the exercise and what you perceive to be the ideal state. The gap analysis would be done by a subset of key stakeholders, process owners, experts, and people who will be affected by changes and improvements. This gap is the most specific, explicit information that can be extracted from a knowledge map. Gap analysis helps prioritize and categorize process information and also ensures your focus remains on critical knowledge. To perform a gap analysis, ask the following questions:

- What critical knowledge is missing?
- What (or who) hinders the flow of knowledge within the process? Why?
- What (or who) enhances the flow of knowledge? Why?
- What are the next steps for the knowledge map? (What is it going to be used for?)

Unlike a global positioning system, the paper road map in your car quickly becomes dated. As your organization changes, your knowledge map will, too. New employees replace outgoing experts, and new goals emerge. Consequently, knowledge mapping is a dynamic, ongoing activity. All knowledge maps need to be reviewed at least annually. Some industries, especially those that are high tech, may require updates every six months. And keep in mind that 20 percent of the information will provide 80 percent of the value. In other words, map the most critical knowledge assets first.

Let's look at an example using an expertise tacit knowledge map. A large regional utility in the southwestern United States had to improve its service restoration process following big storms. Because the organization's service zones covered a densely populated large area, storms could require resources to be marshaled across 60 miles. Thousands of employees could be called upon at any time to coordinate manpower, fix circuits and breakers, report on status, and move equipment.

Our team at APQC helped the organization's service restoration team map the eight main process steps of service restoration, from identifying storm possibilities to returning crews to home service areas. After mapping the process, the group determined what type of expertise was needed during each specific step of the service restoration process. This included things like dispatching, work crew knowledge, district support, and weather reporting.

The group then noted where that expertise existed in each district, be it a single individual or many sharing a specific role. The team rated the levels of expertise of those individuals using their tenure and the number of storm events experienced and then identified significant gap areas. Finally, the team used this knowledge map to develop an invitation list for after-action reviews that pulled in only the appropriate representatives from each process step, region, and group. This resulted in focused meetings with high member satisfaction. As a result of the knowledge mapping, the service restoration realized a 20 percent improvement in reliability in the first year.

Now that you've identified what knowledge is critical, the value proposition and call to action for managing that knowledge, and where critical knowledge resides—or is missing, it helps to understand how that knowledge should flow.

How Knowledge Should Flow

You've found the critical knowledge assets in your organization. How do you make sure this knowledge gets into the right hands?

Use APQC's Knowledge Flow Process to understand how critical knowledge should flow in your organization (see Figure 2.2). The way knowledge flows in organizations is often a hidden process. The purpose of KM is to enable the knowledge flow process, so let's look at each knowledge flow step and the common reasons the process often breaks down to help identify your organization's knowledge gaps and in preparation for designing KM approaches to close those gaps.

- *Create* (sometimes called *innovate* or *invent*). The creation of knowledge happens every day in many different ways such as new experiments, creative implementation plans for new customers, and collaboration around product enhancements.
  - What can go wrong: It is a mistake to narrowly define knowledge creation as something that happens only in the R&D departments. People may not realize they have created

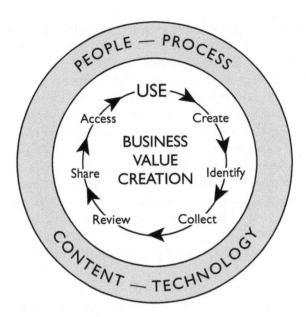

Figure 2.2   APQC's Knowledge Flow Process

knowledge; they are just doing their jobs. Yet, some of it is critical knowledge.

- *Identify (contribute or define).* Locating new or existing knowledge is an important step to keep your focus on only critical knowledge. This is where knowledge maps help.
  - What can go wrong: Those who have the knowledge may not realize others may find it useful. At the same time, those who could benefit from that knowledge may have no idea someone else in the organization already has it. No one is facilitating a link between these two groups.
- *Collect (capture or organize).* This is the process of collecting, capturing, and storing knowledge during an event, such as a team meeting, or in a medium such as a portal, database, or blog.
  - What can go wrong: People may write down too much. Yet, conversely, explicit knowledge doesn't always have the benefit of full context to give it meaning. Additionally, employees cannot always easily locate knowledge sitting in a database that they are not familiar with.

- *Review (evaluate, validate, or analyze).* This is the process of validating or evaluating knowledge for relevance, accuracy, and use.
  - What can go wrong: The lag time between knowledge that is identified and collected and finally validated may cause confusion. There can be a lack of confidence in the knowledge if it has been put in a holding period for review. Also, people can be reluctant to rate, review, or evaluate a knowledge asset.
- *Share (collaborate or publish).* This involves pushing knowledge or information to others, contributing to a group activity or discussion, or responding to questions.
  - What can go wrong: People absorb knowledge from other people they know, respect, and like. If two employees have no personal bond, then they may be less likely to incorporate others' experiences into their own work.
- *Access (find or download).* This is the act of passing a best knowledge asset or expert from one to one or one to many.
  - What can go wrong: Even when employees know about a knowledge asset, they may lack the money, time, relationship, or sponsorship resources to pursue and study it in enough detail to make it useful.
- *Use (transfer, reuse, or adapt or adopt).* Knowledge is taken in its current form and applied to another situation to solve a problem, improve a process, or make a decision.
  - What can go wrong: Personal technical expertise and knowledge creation may be valued over sharing. If the emphasis is on invention rather than adaptation, then employees will not accept knowledge assets from new sources.

By addressing the knowledge flow process at this point, you can assess where the flow of knowledge is breaking down. People who don't know anything about KM suddenly get it when they see how knowledge should flow.

Now that you understand, at a high level, how and what knowledge needs to flow (and from and to whom), you can paint a compelling picture for executives that will give you the buy-in you need to move to the next phases: developing a detailed KM strategy and business case with a portfolio of KM approaches.

Getting Buy-In

If you don't have it already, then you are now ready to ask for permission and for resources to develop or revitalize your KM strategy and create actionable business cases and implementation plans. Call together the executives you interviewed, along with your original sponsor and other stakeholders, to present what you have found as the call to action and what resources and support you need to build a KM strategy. You are asking them to assign and allocate a small number of people to the KM core group and for permission to engage other employees and stakeholders in creating an overarching KM strategy and detailed business cases for where you are going to enable knowledge.

If you have listened well, then you will be able to create a compelling picture—albeit at a high level—of what a better flow of knowledge would mean to them and the organization. This group of supportive senior sponsors and stakeholders may become your KM business leadership group (see Chapter 8).

Closing Comments

An example from IBM GBS illustrates the importance of understanding the value proposition and the critical knowledge your organization has and needs before designing a KM strategy. As IBM's business model moved away from hardware and into solutions and services for its customers, it needed a greater reuse of knowledge about successful solutions, expertise, proposals, and service delivery models. IBM had its KM call to action. Maintaining the skills, knowledge, and talent of consulting and integration employees in IBM GBS was the key to revenue generation for the organization. KM supports IBM's five overarching strategies, especially the fourth one:

1. *Grow the business base.* Increase revenue, win rates, and market share.
2. *Manage profitability.* Increase productivity and time savings, and reuse knowledge assets.
3. *Set the industry bar for quality.* Produce higher quality deliverables and generate increased customer satisfaction with reduced project skills.
4. *Compete based on competencies.* Share knowledge, experiences, and lessons learned, and manage intellectual capital effectively.

5. *Develop brand leadership.* Increase customer satisfaction and loyalty.

Understanding how your organization competes on knowledge can transform the perception and value of KM within your organization, driving tangible results more quickly and avoiding redundant efforts (and investment). Yet, even with the most compelling value proposition, we never forget that knowledge is sticky. It won't move without help. Now that you know what knowledge is critical and how it should flow, you need a systematic KM strategy and the right approaches to make it flow.

Implementation Resources

This chapter details all the pertinent considerations for your call to action. The following APQC resources can help you further explore this topic:

- *Ensuring that Communities Fulfill Explicit Business Objectives*
- *Identifying Critical Knowledge: An APQC Overview*
- *Knowledge Map and Process Map Overview*
- *Knowledge Mapping: The Essentials for Success*
- *Knowledge: How Much Is Too Much?*
- *The Executive's Role in Knowledge Management*
- APQC Training: *Knowledge Mapping*
- APQC Training: *Process Mapping*

These resources—along with APQC's custom advisory services and more than 1,000 articles focused on KM—are available at www.apqc.org and through this book's Web site at www.newedgeinknowledge.com.

3

Knowledge Management Strategy and Business Case

At this point, you have a clear value proposition and call to action to help knowledge flow. Now you are ready to develop (or revitalize) your enterprise KM strategy to do just that. In the process, you will develop a business case to attract resources, involvement, and sponsorship. The strategy clarifies who the various KM sponsors are and where the program and approaches funding will come from. Essentially, it's your plan to proceed.

This chapter discusses how to develop your KM strategy and business case. It also addresses how to design a strategy that can quickly build on existing KM capabilities rather than starting from scratch, using APQC's levels of knowledge management maturity.[1]

An Enterprise KM Program versus Local Initiatives

There's a good reason this book focuses on organization-wide KM efforts: It's the best way to achieve significant results, now and in the long term. An enterprise KM program spans the various organization silos, builds a common way of working, avoids redundant efforts, and leads to more reuse of knowledge in new and innovative ways.

Enterprise KM programs are quite different from local KM initiatives in regard to dynamics and potential. An enterprise KM program has many sponsors and therefore serves many masters. Although this adds complexity in design and change management, all of these inputs drive a more strategically

(Continued)

focused KM program, with more efficiently scaled efforts and less confusion from conflicting standards or expectations and competing tools.

Another benefit of starting a KM program with an enterprise perspective is the variety of prototypes that can be tested to fit the range of possible environments. This makes for far richer and more varied findings about what KM will look like in your environment and creates more advocates across your organization. The resulting solutions are more robust and make going to scale far easier.

Finally, an enterprise approach can make a far stronger case for investing in KM activities (the supporting people, pilots, training, content, and technology) than can a local effort, which will serve fewer people and needs.

A Framework for KM Strategy Development

APQC's Levels of Knowledge Management Maturity (see Figure 3.1) is a framework to ensure that you include all the important elements in your KM strategy. It is also an assessment tool that can tell you what capabilities you have and give you milestones to gauge your progress. Each level identifies characteristics, tasks, and the kind of

Figure 3.1   APQC's Levels of Knowledge Management Maturity

results you would expect to see if your KM program was operating at that level of maturity.

The levels are based on our experience with countless KM programs over the years and have been validated through testing. The framework's great value provides a clear assessment of your current KM capabilities at the point of program development.

We use the APQC KM Capability and Assessment Tool to help organizations validate and target their programs' issues, gaps, and strengths. Figure 3.2 illustrates how we can gauge your level of maturity in terms of objectives, business case, budget, resources, governance and leadership, change management, communication, knowledge flow process, KM approaches, measurement, content management, and IT. This information can help you understand the current overall capabilities of your KM program and what specific areas need attention in order for it to mature. (Visit www.newedgeinknowledge.com to find out how to complete the APQC KM Capability and Assessment Tool.)

We find that KM practitioners often get sidetracked by focusing intently on only one category and thinking the others will follow

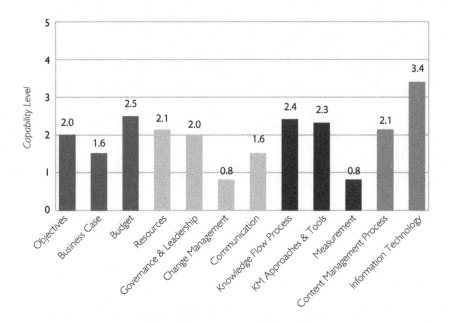

Figure 3.2   KM Capability Assessment Overview: Twelve KM Capabilities

suit. Your KM strategy must effectively delineate resources across all of these categories of concern to engage employees in KM approaches and results. The assessment tool points out areas that could be holding your program back. For example, the organization featured in Figure 3.2 is noteworthy for the relatively high maturity of their IT compared to change management and measurement. Despite investments in IT, the KM program leadership has not sufficiently measured and communicated gains from initiatives to date. They may be getting great results, but these results are invisible to decision makers. If they work on those gaps in change management and measurement, then they could begin to reap significant benefits.

The following sections show how this framework can give you a clear sense of strengths, gaps, and opportunities for improvement to help you develop a KM strategy appropriate for your organization's level of KM maturity.

How Knowledge Use Matures with Your Program

As your KM capabilities mature, so will your ability to apply knowledge to add value. The nature of your critical knowledge will evolve as your KM program progresses through the maturity levels portrayed in Figure 3.1:

- *Ad hoc knowledge.* Knowledge is inconsistently captured, and awareness of its reuse is low within the organization.
- *Applied knowledge.* There is recognition of the value of organizational knowledge, leading to interest in more consistent reuse.
- *Leveraged knowledge.* Knowledge and its flow is a key enabler of organizational performance.
- *Dynamic knowledge.* Knowledge is used as a competitive differentiator as well as an enabler of innovation and is applied pervasively throughout the organization.

Characteristics and Focus at Each Level

Table 3.1 is a short description of what you can expect to see at each maturity level.

KM Strategy Focus

Now that you have a clear sense of strengths, gaps, and opportunities for improvement, how do you spell out your KM strategy's objectives?

Table 3.1   Maturity Level Characteristics

Characteristics and Focus	Description
Level 1—Initiate: Growing awareness At maturity level 1, your organization is aware that it has a problem retaining and sharing knowledge.	Your organization has identified a need to assess its situation, and senior leaders support testing a KM proof of concept or creating a KM strategy. At this level, the KM leader will assess the current state in knowledge sharing, potential barriers to sharing knowledge and competing issues, and existing technologies and tools that can be leveraged as needed.
Level 2—Develop: **Growing Involvement** At maturity level 2, initial knowledge approaches are in place. The focus is on helping localized knowledge flow and add value.	Your organization has identified improvement opportunities, and a KM core group is establishing a strategic direction. The group works to identify critical knowledge, conduct a needs assessment with IT and other relevant employee groups, develop key performance indicators for initial KM efforts, and provide knowledge maps to address knowledge needs and gaps.
Level 3—Standardize: Aligning **processes and approaches** At maturity level 3, the knowledge flow processes are standardized and the focus is on meeting organizational requirements, achieving results, and developing a supporting infrastructure.	Your organization has standard knowledge flow processes, replicable KM approaches, and supporting tools. It has begun to see measurable results from its initial KM efforts, which have strategic ownership and a core KM group with defined roles and responsibilities. Your organization's infrastructure supports enterprise KM efforts, and a scorecard monitors the health and effectiveness of KM efforts.
Level 4—Optimize: Driving **organizational outcomes** At maturity level 4, the KM efforts align with your organization's objectives and the focus is on leveraging core knowledge assets across the enterprise.	KM capabilities enable your organization to leverage knowledge in support of its mission. KM is treated as a core function. The KM strategy integrates with enterprise strategy, and KM reporting processes align with enterprise reporting. KM responsibilities factor into individual performance assessments and are part of talent management and leader development programs.

(Continued)

Table 3.1 *(Continued)*

Characteristics and Focus	Description
Level 5—Innovate: Continually improving practices At maturity level 5, KM practices are embedded in key processes and the focus is on the competency of your organization.	Your organization's knowledge flow supports innovation and continuous improvement. KM is part of an enterprise excellence framework, and standard budgeting processes help managers obtain the funding they need to continually improve their efforts. The KM group works with vendors and internal groups responsible for talent management, leader development, process improvement, and organizational learning to develop new uses of KM output that will improve enterprise effectiveness.

Your value proposition and understanding of critical knowledge will drive your KM program strategy objectives. Common objectives include:

- Bringing new hires up to speed more quickly
- Capturing valuable knowledge as employees leave
- Capturing project lessons learned for reuse
- Preventing the loss of technical knowledge
- Expanding innovative capabilities
- Building a knowledge-sharing culture
- Accelerating the rate of learning for all employees
- Providing inexperienced employees access to more experienced employees

You then focus on effectively delineating resources to establish and improve your KM capabilities in regard to people, processes, and technology.

In terms of people, your strategy should specify expectations for the KM program to communicate, promote, and educate employees about the KM approach. It should lay out the centralized infrastructure that will support all KM approaches. It should also specify expectations for the KM program to engage, recognize, and reward those who lead and participate in KM activities. This is an often neglected but extremely critical element of your KM strategy.

In terms of processes, your strategy should provide criteria for selecting KM approaches to manage high-value tacit knowledge. Using KM approaches that are inherently rewarding to participants is the objective. The strategy should specify indicators and measures of success for KM approaches, tools, and projects to facilitate their alignment with overall strategic goals.

In terms of technology, your strategy should provide guidance for a common set of IT tools to support KM approaches and activities. Creating processes that identify, collect, categorize, and refresh content using a common taxonomy across your organization serves as a foundation for the knowledge flow processes required. The strategy should specify expectations for the KM program to help employees find information, find people, and answer questions.

By addressing all of these factors in your KM strategy, you have the necessary components for a strong business case.

Balancing Strategic Concerns

Whenever possible, we encourage you to leverage existing enterprise IT tools rather than incur incremental technology costs. Spend your money facilitating the processes and the people.

The Business Case for KM

When APQC started studying KM in its early stages, a KM program might get launched and funded on vision and promise. But in a climate of ever-increasing emphasis on productivity and effectiveness, KM is not exempt from scrutiny. Your KM strategy must illustrate a solid business case that demonstrates value and a deep understanding of your organization's critical knowledge needs.

The value proposition you determined in Chapter 2 is the vision and rationale to manage the flow of critical knowledge. The business case, on the other hand, designates action. It forces you to provide an estimate of what the potential investment and resource requirements will be to make knowledge flow where it needs to. It's what allows you to formalize your KM program and sustain KM approaches.

Your business case should include:

- Initial scope (process, project, function, or knowledge domain)
- Goals, objectives, and key performance indicators for initial scope
- Background information
- Opportunities for better knowledge flow including benefits and value
- Resource and IT requirements
- Sponsors and key stakeholders
- Risks and barriers to success
- Estimated costs and benefits
- Milestones and potential time line
- Approval to proceed

You *could* build a business case for KM approaches at a local level, but that would not help build enterprise capacity for the future. You need a foundation for replicable models to build ever more powerful capacity for the future challenges your organization will face. And you need to avoid the costs of redundant efforts and design work. ("Design once, use again" is a mantra of the best KM programs.) Make the business case for an enterprise KM program with standard KM approaches, not a loose collection of local, unscalable KM initiatives. Your employees will appreciate the consistent approaches. Underfunding KM by forcing it to start locally will lead to underwhelming results and what APQC chairman Jack Grayson likes to call "random acts of improvement."

Also, be careful that the initial value proposition for enabling knowledge flow doesn't get lost in a perfect strategy with a lot of proposed infrastructure built above employees' work flow. It is true that you can build capabilities faster when you are not trying to embed them into the daily work flow, but it is risky to believe that they can stay above the work flow and still become part of the fabric and culture of how your organization works.

A business case takes time and critical thinking about the value of knowledge assets. Not every opportunity you uncover will require this type of due diligence. So as you gather the data needed to complete the business cases within the scope of your opportunities, combine your knowledge strategy criteria with KM criteria to evaluate the information and assumptions. It's important to develop a deeper understanding of your organization's critical knowledge assets—how they flow and their potential impact. It will save you time, money, and frustration.

Ask yourself: Does our business case draw a line to tangible results? Does it leverage existing infrastructures, including IT tools? Does it set the stage for replicable methodologies and common processes? And most importantly, does it spell out how KM will serve our organization's overall strategic goals?

The importance of providing business value cannot be underestimated; most organizations will require KM to clearly articulate business value and link to business objectives. With the resources that come from a successful KM strategy and business case, you will be ready to adopt KM approaches to address the knowledge needs and create knowledge flows.

Closing Comments

Keep in mind these five basic tenets of a KM strategy:

1. *The KM strategy is based on balancing people, process, and technology concerns.* Each element needs enablers and capabilities to help critical knowledge move throughout your organization.
2. *The KM strategy contributes to overall organizational goals.* Focus on identifying and supporting knowledge flows around critical processes. Taking a more systematic approach to managing knowledge will contribute to bottom-line objectives. Balance instances of immediate impact and long-term needs.
3. *Timing is everything.* Your KM strategy should identify the sequencing of key activities and building capabilities that will help build the overall infrastructure and demonstrate organizational value sooner rather than later.
4. *The KM strategy leverages common processes and technology.* Value is gained from the application of KM across the enterprise, leveraging a common knowledge flow process enabled by standard IT tools. Support collaboration within and among business units and functions.
5. *The strategy will transform the perception and value of KM.* If your KM strategy is successful, then it will show results, avoid redundancy and duplication of effort (and investment), and enhance competitiveness.

Armed with these basic tenets, you are ready to select the appropriate battery of KM approaches.

Implementation Resources

This chapter discusses the formation of a KM strategy and business case. The following APQC resources can help you further explore this topic:

- APQC's Levels of Knowledge Management Maturity
- APQC's Knowledge Management Capability Assessment Tool
- *Key Elements of a Knowledge Management Business Case*
- "The Role of Knowledge Management in Innovation," Carla O'Dell's presentation from APQC's 2007 KM Conference
- *Using Business Cases to Establish a Knowledge Management Framework*
- *Using Communities of Practice to Respond to Strategic Drivers*
- *Where Are You Now? A KM Program Self-Assessment*

These resources—along with APQC's custom advisory services and more than 1,000 articles focused on KM—are available at www.apqc.org and through this book's Web site at www.newedgeinknowledge.com.

Note

1. The first version of the APQC's Levels of Knowledge Management Maturity was piloted by APQC with support from its 2008 KM Advanced Working Group.

CHAPTER 4

Selecting and Designing Knowledge Management Approaches

Once you have a call to action *(ready)* and a KM strategy and business case *(aim)*, you are then ready to put approaches in place to support the flow of critical knowledge *(fire)*. KM program development is about designing and launching these approaches.

As shown in Chapters 2 and 3, the analysis that led to your understanding of your organization's strategic knowledge needs, as well as the pressing gaps or opportunities, will help focus your KM approaches on the right group of employees and issues. A KM core group can take the KM strategy and turn it into robust, repeatable, and stable approaches. The goals are to address the immediate problems and build long-term capabilities at the same time.

This chapter introduces categories of KM approaches to consider and then shares examples and key advice to select and design the right approaches.

A Portfolio of Approaches

We have seen and used many approaches among APQC's customers and members to help knowledge flow. The biggest mistake KM core groups make is thinking that a single approach will solve their problems when, in fact, it often requires a portfolio of approaches working in concert to address all of the knowledge needs. Some approaches are people-intensive, and others rely more heavily on technology. Most KM approaches fall into one or more of four categories: self-service, lessons learned, communities of practice, and the facilitated transfer of best practices (see Figure 4.1).

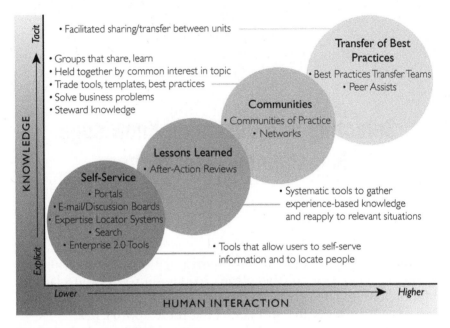

Figure 4.1   Categories of KM Approaches

The categories of approaches vary by how much they focus on explicit and tacit knowledge and how much human interaction or facilitation is involved.

1. *Self-service.* This technology-focused category of KM approaches enables access to information and codified knowledge from dialogue and discussion. Think of intranets, role-based portals, people finders, and search tools sustained by comprehensive content management systems. The objective of self-service approaches is to link your employees at their desktop or work site to the knowledge assets they need to do their job more effectively. The focus is on enabling your employees to help themselves at the teachable moment while in the work flow. Virtually every enterprise KM program will have a self-service approach in its portfolio.

2. *Lessons learned.* Applied to specific processes and projects, this category of KM approaches helps employees capture, share, and reuse lessons based on their experiences. Also known as after-action reviews, lessons learned is a category of KM

approaches in which the participants debrief major events to capture lessons, best practices, and understand factors of success or failure so they can take corrective action or avoid making the same mistake again. An additional goal is to share these lessons with colleagues who can benefit in their situation. Lessons-learned approaches can benefit any organization, but they have special power in high-stakes sectors in which mistakes can cost lives such as military, emergency response, aerospace and defense, heavy mining, and oil and gas.

3. *Communities of practice.* Communities—sometimes called networks—consist of employees who come together face to face and virtually around an issue, discipline, or body of knowledge to share and learn from one another. They tend to be formal; have a common goal and a desire to share experiences, insights, and best practices; shepherd a body of knowledge; and professionally develop their members. With the advantage of crossing formal organizational boundaries, communities of practice are probably the most ubiquitous KM approach. They are the foundation of virtually every mature KM program we have seen.

4. *The facilitated transfer of best practices.* The facilitated transfer of best practices involves identifying and transferring successful, demonstrated practices and processes among units in an organization. The value proposition is to close performance gaps and bring all similar organizational units up to the same level of high performance. A systematic and robust transfer process usually involves formal facilitation and coaching through a structured methodology (if the process or practice is complex). This KM approach provides the highest measurable monetary gains because it focuses on the implementation of proven practices. It achieves especially high gains in organizations whose operating units perform similar activities (e.g., retail and manufacturing) or where there needs to be a standard global process across all operating units (e.g., engineering, construction, and financial services.)

Some KM approaches, such as communities of practice, have proven themselves over the years and have well-established methodologies and best practices. Other, emerging approaches such as social networking and wikis have exciting potential. (We examine both in greater detail in the following chapters.)

A Word about Collaboration Tools

There are many information technology (IT) and enterprise applications such as Microsoft SharePoint and virtual conferencing that can be put to good use in KM, especially supporting self-service and communities of practice. But using these tools is not the same as having a KM approach. For example, you don't need a KM program to have project team spaces, conduct Webinars and team meetings, or use other means of connecting employees. The distinction we make is that KM programs are systematic and facilitated processes to help specific knowledge flow, achieve specific outcomes, and grow specific capabilities over time.

Selecting KM Approaches

So, what will best serve your organization? You will likely need a combination of KM approaches. There is a continuous tension and balancing act between the need for IT and the need to focus on people. We believe it is best in this balancing act to lean to the people side. After all, employees are the sources and recipients of all knowledge and the reason we have organizations in the first place.

The following questions can help you think through the nature of the target opportunity—your organization's employees and the critical knowledge assets—and which KM approaches will best serve your organization's needs.

1. Is the critical knowledge currently tacit or explicit?
2. What is the nature of the knowledge conversion required?
   • From tacit to explicit
   • Tacit to tacit
   • Explicit to tacit
   • Explicit to explicit
3. What is the nature and pace of the work?
   • Scientific and technical (e.g., engineering and research)
   • Customer-facing (e.g., sales)
   • Problem-solving (e.g., help desks)

- Design
- Production

4. What are the existing relationships among the target employees? Do they know each other? Is there an existing network or group you can leverage?
5. What other characteristics of the employees and work affect knowledge flows?
    - Cultural, regional, and language differences
    - Experience in collaboration
6. Can you leverage existing tools? What is your familiarity with the IT options? What tools are people using now?
7. What resources are available to support the initiation and maintenance of the approach?
    - Business unit involvement
    - Central KM resources
8. Is there a crisis or are you building long-term capability?
9. What outcomes are you seeking? What does success need to look like in what time frame? Are there existing business measures that would improve as a result?

The answers to these questions paint a picture of the people and knowledge involved as well as the resources upon which your KM program can draw. For example, if the nature of the work is scientific and technical and the target group is scientists who want to talk about research issues and problems, then setting up opportunities for dialogue will be part of your design. In addition, if they already have technical forms in which they participate, then you could help capture more of the tacit knowledge shared at those events. A community of practice could meet virtually between these meetings to continue the dialogue around important issues. Furthermore, they may wish to have better access to more of their documents and past research, as well as the ability to recommend other content to one another. You can begin to see how this information reveals which KM approaches to use.

It is important to note that the first two questions are central knowledge issues. Ikujiro Nonaka and Hirotaka Takeuchi best illustrated how dynamic knowledge switches between tacit and explicit with their four modes of knowledge (Nonaka and Takeuchi 1995). We've adapted their model in Figure 4.2. Imagine the quadrant in which critical knowledge and employees—your recipients of critical

Figure 4.2   Converting Critical Knowledge Types

Adapted from Ikujiro Nonaka and Hirotaka Takeuchi, *The Knowledge-Creating Company: How Japanese Companies Create the Dynamics of Innovation.* New York: Oxford University Press, 1995.

knowledge—are now, what form of knowledge it is, and what form it needs to be when the knowledge flow cycle is complete.

The later questions help evaluate how ambitious your KM program can be and how to measure results. For each specific approach you consider, perform this value path thought experiment to simulate how the process is supposed to work. Imagine the following:

- In what very specific circumstances would employees use the approach?
- What do you expect them to do?
- Then what would happen? And what do you expect the result to be?
- When are teachable moments likely to occur? Where will the employees likely be when it happens? How would they reach out for help or ideas?

The KM strategy requires that two perspectives and levels of approaches be served here: *above the flow* and *in the flow* of work.

1. *Above the flow.* Your KM core group should build the core capabilities (in IT, approaches, change management, communications, branding, measurement, etc.) that will become the infrastructure and foundation of your entire KM program. Creating and maintaining this infrastructure is above the flow of work. It is foundational and strategic. Also, the KM core group needs to build a portfolio of approaches that are scalable and replicable across multiple locations and circumstances. Communities of practice are a good example; if you develop a robust approach to chartering communities, training leaders, enlisting and sustaining participation, and capturing wins, then you can standardize and package this to happen over and over again. You will get a more consistent result at a much lower cost. (Of course, there will be times a crisis or a specific need justifies the creation of a unique approach that may not be used again.)

2. *In the flow.* Your KM core group and design teams (see Chapter 8) should design KM approaches to fit the flow of knowledge in employees' everyday work. The KM program should ensure that approaches respond to the teachable moment in the flow of work as much as possible.

Consider the KM approaches selected by Schlumberger. It has given its employees access to Eureka communities of practice and the Schlumberger InTouch system, which is a 24/7 technical help desk to help field service employees at their most teachable moment. The Eureka communities are focused on either a discipline, a problem, or on accessing expert input. The InTouch system helps employees find validated information about Schlumberger products and services, such as manuals, training materials, technical updates, alerts, solutions, best practices, and lessons learned.

Schlumberger weaves the sharing and reuse of knowledge into people's work flow so that it is a normal, natural part of the job. Schlumberger believes that by embedding KM into people's routine work (i.e., in the flow), they enable employees to be more innovative, create new business, increase quality and efficiency, decrease time to competency, and generally make better, faster decisions.

Designing a KM Approach

Based on our experience designing KM approaches with many of APQC's clients, we've compiled the following high-level overview of the key design principles that apply to every KM approach. In later chapters, we point out issues related to specific approaches.

- Before you design a specific KM approach, establish an executive champion, a design team, a strong project leader or facilitator, and involve embedded knowledge managers in the process or knowledge domain.
- Create scalable approaches and replicable infrastructure.
- Secure resources and support at both enterprise and local levels to drive consistency and sustainability for each approach. Local funding provides contextual resources for the approach. Enterprise or centralized funding provides infrastructure.
- Make each approach inherently rewarding to use. Realize it may change the way employees are currently working, so there needs to be a compelling reason to switch.
- Pilot the approaches and their measures. Allow cycles of learning and experimentation. And look for the lessons that reside in failed attempts. Embedding knowledge flow using KM approaches takes time, mentoring, and cycles of practice.
- Even if you decide to initially launch a KM approach in just one part of your organization, anticipate the biggest eventual scale because the KM strategy needs to be designed accordingly. Benchmarking with other KM programs or using the APQC KM Capability Assessment Tool can give you a sense of the scale that your enterprise program will require.
- There will always be a new technology. Don't try to design the perfect IT solution. Get the people and processes right, and you can find IT that will work.
- Focus on breaking down structural barriers to the flow of knowledge between employees who have it and those who need it—not on changing the culture. Common structural barriers include a lack of time, a cumbersome process, and employees who do not know where to find information, whom to talk to, or whether they can trust the information. Work on these barriers rather than on the psychological makeup of your employees.

- Make it fun. Brand it.
- Determine how and where to embed the approach into the flow of work itself; look for teachable moments.
- And finally, don't forget that all approaches require governance, change management strategies, and measures of involvement and impact.

Chapters 8, 9, and 10 help you drill down into the specifics of this advice.

What Can Go Wrong

Don't start with approaches at the extreme ends of tacit or explicit knowledge. As every tennis player knows, the sweet spot lies in the middle of the racket.

At one end of the spectrum is the explicit nature of Big IT, in which the main focus is the design and deployment of large, enterprise IT applications. These approaches enable everything; but without a specific problem to solve and a change management strategy, not much happens. Technology applications do not, in themselves, motivate employees to share knowledge or to change behavior. Technology is indispensable to KM in large organizations, but it must be part of a systematic KM strategy.

For years, we saw these IT initiatives start with a lot of hope and investment and then crash and burn when it became painfully obvious that no one was using the tools. Many an early chief knowledge officer's career met its demise from a big IT implementation. "If you build it, they will not necessarily come" became a famous tag line in the early days of KM, and everyone knew that it meant an IT solution without a problem or a constituency clamoring for it.

We couldn't understand why smart people continued to make that mistake. Then we realized why: IT is tangible. You either have it or you don't. You know when you have rolled it out. It sounds like a *solution*. It is something you can describe and sell. And let's face it: IT can be dazzling. We have noticed that some of the best KM programs make such creative use of IT applications—MITRE and IBM are two that easily come to mind—that those who benchmark them don't notice the "man behind the curtain." The real wizardry lies in their intense focus on letting employees take the lead on design; strong processes; communication, change management, and building support for the tool; and branding, videos, and campaigns to make it fun.

The best way to embed knowledge into day-to-day organizational life is to involve employees in developing the knowledge flow that supports their work and fits their culture. Employees usually support what they help create. IBM and MITRE are masters at engaging their employees in prototyping approaches.

At the other extreme, softer tacit-to-tacit approaches (e.g., a learning organization, mentoring, or employee development) in the name of KM can be too soft and fuzzy for embryonic KM programs to show results. We would get calls from leaders of some of the best organizations in the world, frustrated that they couldn't get any traction with "the learning organization" as their mantra. It didn't seem to have a concrete methodology or a tangible, urgent, and measurable problem it was designed to fix. You couldn't tell whether you were making progress or not. And it blended too much into the woodwork. Ironically, it was so embedded in the work flow that you couldn't even see it.

Of course, for mature enterprise KM programs, tacit-to-tacit approaches can be profoundly impactful. By then, you will have bought the time and space to focus KM on the harder and more rewarding work of tacit-to-tacit knowledge creation (Nonaka 1995).

This is not to say you shouldn't buy IT solutions or develop a mentoring program if that is what your gap analysis indicates is the right approach. Just be mindful that it is risky to base your whole KM strategy on this if you don't make it tangible and create a measurable business case and indicators of progress that leaders care about. Identifying the capabilities you need is the fun part; getting the right resources and budget to support them is the hard part.

To illustrate the key points in this chapter, the following section is an example of a portfolio of approaches to a common KM call to action: to capture and retain critical knowledge over time.

Portfolio Example: Retaining Critical Knowledge

One of the most common calls to action for KM programs is retaining critical knowledge before it walks out the door. Today's most pervasive knowledge issues result from the constant movement of employees from project to project inside organizations, as well as the entrance of new employees as others leave. Your KM strategy will most likely at some point need to address knowledge retention factors such as rapid organizational growth, waves of retirement from baby boomers, layoffs, turnover, mergers and acquisitions, and internal redeployments. Many organizations faced with these challenges struggle to balance crisis approaches such as exit interviews with long-term interventions such as content harvesting. Let's examine best-practice approaches for this KM challenge.

A Strategic Opportunity

APQC's open standards benchmarking research indicates that less than half of respondents to its "Redeploy and Retire Employees" benchmarking survey have a knowledge retention plan in place for employees approaching retirement.

A Strategic Focus

In APQC's study *Retaining Valuable Knowledge*, we gauged how organizations identify, capture, and retain critical knowledge. As you might suspect, we found that the best way to retain knowledge is to build strategic KM approaches in advance of the problem.

In APQC's study *Retaining Today's Knowledge for Tomorrow's Work Force*, we then examined how leading organizations mitigate the loss of critical knowledge. They, in fact, view the processes of pinpointing knowledge and ascertaining who has it as intrinsically related. They use the same approaches for both purposes, although with a slightly different emphasis, depending on whether they are locating knowledge or knowledge owners.

By determining what knowledge is critical to your organization, you have already identified what knowledge is most important to retain. Spelling out your knowledge retention needs through your KM strategy can help you now find the most appropriate KM approaches to capture and transfer knowledge. The most common efforts to retain knowledge involve:

- Building a knowledge-sharing culture
- Capturing and using lessons learned
- Capturing valuable knowledge for transfer and reuse as employees leave

- Developing employees' skills by providing access to more experienced or knowledgeable employees
- Performing succession planning
- Preventing the loss of knowledge related to organizational culture
- Preventing the loss of technical knowledge
- Retaining valuable knowledge as employees transfer from one job to another inside an organization

It's also important to note that knowledge retention approaches are boosted by being aligned with your organization's human capital management function. In fact, elements of human capital management architecture often drive KM approaches to retain knowledge. By forming relationships with other groups—such as quality, organizational development, HR/personnel development, training, and IT functions—you can broaden the reach of your efforts, thereby increasing the number of employees touched and the amount of knowledge retained.

Fluor's Knowledge Loss Risk Assessment

Fluor's assessment is distinct in the way it determines the impact of retirement and resource gaps, particularly for the organization's subject matter expertise. Adapted from the Tennessee Valley Authority model, the formula multiplies the retirement factor against the position risk factor to determine the total attrition factor. This approach helps integrate KM with human capital management by identifying where expertise (and therefore knowledge) may be at risk and by effectively communicating the impact of potential knowledge loss and priorities. Fluor's network leaders are then in a position to hire or train to mitigate the risks of loss.

Knowledge Retention: A Portfolio of Approaches

We've found that best-practice organizations leverage an array of KM approaches designed to fit specific organizational concerns and the unique cultures of their respective organizations in order to retain knowledge. They tend to embed their knowledge retention efforts into their work flows by balancing short-term, urgent needs based on looming retirement with the long-term vision of their KM strategies. Here are the most popular approaches that span the employment life cycle:

- *Communities of practice.* Communities are *the* core tool to capture and transfer critical knowledge. Committed and accountable community leaders play a key role in retaining knowledge.
- *Transfer of job-related knowledge.* A transfer approach can capture critical knowledge related to a specific job or role through audits, hand-off documents, lessons learned, and structured interviews.
- *Mentoring and apprenticeship programs.* In the past few years, we've noticed a resurgence in mentoring and apprenticeship programs. Traditionally, these programs have focused on leadership, behavioral, and skill development. However, they can also be used as a means of transferring tacit knowledge from a more experienced employee to a more junior employee, especially in technical and engineering domains where talent is often in short supply.
- *Structured use of subject matter experts.* Over the years, subject matter experts have come to play a key, if somewhat ad hoc, role in KM because of their ability to answer questions, provide historical perspective, offer solutions, and so on. In knowledge retention efforts, their role becomes more formal and structured.
- *Storytelling programs.* Stories can supply context for successes and lessons learned, and each story has the potential to personalize an issue by bringing it alive for its audience. Stories are also an effective way to bridge generational gaps, communicate important information about an organization's culture, and help employees develop a sense of organizational identity.
- *Partnerships with in-house training organizations.* Traditionally, training functions are solely responsible for helping employees develop their skills and capabilities. However, best-practice organizations often have training functions and KM programs collaborate in knowledge retention approaches.
- *Leveraging retirees.* Knowledge retention does not stop with retirement. Retirees can provide needed skills and experience on specific projects, mentor junior employees, and participate

in storytelling and training activities that allow them to share their experiences.

Other examples of approaches include after-action reviews; best practices portals; online collaboration workspaces; technical research reports, papers, and presentations; decision support systems; expertise locator systems; internal conferences to promote knowledge sharing; lessons-learned exercises; new-employee transfer induction programs; peer assists; and project milestone reviews.

Best-Practice Examples

Let's examine how best-practice organizations select KM approaches to address their knowledge retention needs.

Knowledge retention has been a top priority for the Aerospace Corporation since its founding in 1960. Most of the programs in which Aerospace is involved go on for decades, making knowledge retention critical in the face of rapid staff turnover at customer organizations. The types of knowledge that are critical to retain within the technical and programmatic areas of the organization are also the elements that are most valued by Aerospace's customers.

The Aerospace knowledge retention strategy is organization-wide and integrates with both its KM strategy and its workforce planning strategy. Aerospace's KM office is charged with leading a KM subcouncil that coordinates KM approaches through a customer council, whose members represent a cross-section of business interests throughout the organization.

Aerospace has dealt with the challenges of retaining and transferring key knowledge through:

- The development of intensive content and document management resources and systems
- A governance and organizational structure aligned with knowledge needs
- The acculturation and orientation of new employees
- A robust and long-standing retiree work program
- A strong focus on communities of practice in engineering and programs to cut across the organizational structure

In another example, Michelin North America's low turnover has made the baby boomer retirement issue particularly acute within its workforce. The nature of the organization's products is highly specialized, and the required skills are not generally available from the outside, so developing and retaining knowledge is critical to the organization's success. In 2003, to address workforce concerns, Michelin adopted a formal knowledge retention strategy as part of an overall, systematic global knowledge and workforce strategy.

Michelin has four expertise areas. Each expertise area has an overall director of performance and a designated director of competencies. The directors of competencies establish communities of practice across the organization to achieve their mission. In support of these areas, Michelin designed and deployed formal approaches for capturing and transferring tacit and explicit knowledge. The approaches include videotaped, structured interviews that become full-text indexed and searchable, and hand-off documents with structured checklists that capture basic information about employees' jobs in order to guide the employees' replacements.

In a final example, NASA's mission is to pioneer the future in space exploration, scientific discovery, and aeronautics research. The challenges of new missions, combined with the failures of certain missions, budget cuts, and an aging workforce forced NASA to realize the potential for the loss of valuable knowledge. As a result, NASA instituted a formal knowledge retention strategy that is part of its overall systematic KM strategy and workforce planning strategy.

The key objectives of NASA's KM efforts are to sustain NASA's knowledge across missions and generations; help employees find, organize, and share the knowledge that they already have; and increase collaboration while facilitating knowledge creation and sharing. This is accomplished by identifying and capturing the information that exists across the agency, efficiently managing the agency's knowledge resources, and developing techniques and tools to enable teams and communities to collaborate.

Closing Comments

No KM program has to start with a blank sheet of paper. There is an extensive body of experience and best practices available through APQC and others about how to design and implement these approaches in the context of a KM strategy. With our main focus in this book on strategy, we won't try to repeat all of those implementation factors here. Instead, we use the remainder of the book to share and illustrate the most essential—and sometimes counterintuitive—findings and methods of the world-class organizations with which we work. We introduce you to several more examples as we move deeper into the approaches and principles of a successful and sustainable KM strategy.

Implementation Resources

The following APQC resources can help you design and implement your KM approaches:

- APQC's Open Standards Benchmarking Assessments: *Human Capital Management*
- *Assessing Culture and Readiness to Execute Communities of Practice*
- *Capturing Critical Knowledge from a Shifting Workforce*
- *Form Follows Function: Design and Launch Effective Communities of Practice*
- *Key Approaches for Knowledge Retention and Transfer*
- *Measuring the Impact of Knowledge Management*
- *Retaining Today's Knowledge for Tomorrow's Workforce*
- *Retaining Valuable Knowledge: Proactive Strategies to Deal with a Shifting Workforce*
- *Selecting the Right Collaboration Tools*
- APQC Training: *Building and Sustaining Communities of Practice*

These resources—along with APQC's custom advisory services and more than 1,000 articles focused on KM—are available at www.apqc.org and through this book's Web site at www.newedgeinknowledge.com.

5

Proven Knowledge Management Approaches

There will always be new applications, new approaches, and new pitches in the KM arena. But we can't let you forget the foundational KM approaches with proven track records. KM is an established discipline because of the significant results brought by long-standing approaches. By using proven practices, you reduce your risks and accelerate your implementation. Take advantage of the lessons learned by early adopters, use implementation guides based on best practices, and use their successes as proof in your own business case.

This chapter examines in greater detail the power of now-traditional KM approaches: communities of practice, lessons learned, and the facilitated transfer of best practices. They have proven over time to produce stable and measurable organizational benefits.

Communities of Practice

Communities of practice are KM's killer application. This approach most comprehensively addresses the raison d'être of KM: connecting employees to get answers at a teachable moment, collecting content important to a community of employees, retaining content when employees leave the community, and keeping content fresh by capturing ongoing dialogue. Consider communities to be boundary-spanning units responsible for finding and sharing best practices, stewarding knowledge, and helping employees work better. Communities are important because they nurture and harness the raw material of this millennium—knowledge—in the service of your organization.

What can communities do for your organization? Through more than a decade of APQC research and experience, we have found that communities:

- Provide the means to translate local know-how into global, collective knowledge
- Help employees exchange ideas, collaborate, and learn from one another
- Transcend boundaries created by work flow, functions, geography, and time
- Enable the speed and innovation needed for marketplace leadership
- Can integrate into the fabric of your organization's core work and value chains
- Can successfully align with formal governance structures

At an individual level, communities help employees form relationships that provide social support, excitement, and personal validation. Members collaborate, use one another as sounding boards, teach each other, and strike out together to explore relevant subject matter. In our sometimes large and far-flung organizations, the sense of belonging to a community can mean a lot to employees.

Fluor's Success

Almost 100 percent of the Fluor targeted workforce is now actively involved in one or more communities, connecting with their colleagues, sharing knowledge globally, enabling work processes, and bringing new people up to speed quickly.

It's important to note that communities of practice also reveal best practices. Tips and ideas come out of communities all the time. Community members can identify the promising ones, and experts can determine which ideas demonstrably improve a process or problem and validate those that should be adopted by everyone (see Figure 5.1).

Numerous findings and statistics from APQC's studies attest to the deep penetration of communities into the mainstream of many

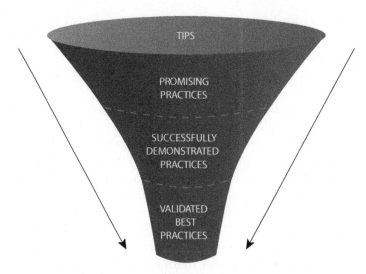

Figure 5.1   The Continuum of Knowledge Shared in Communities of Practice

organizations. In APQC's study *Building and Sustaining Communities of Practice,* we predicted that communities would become the locus for identifying, sharing, and creating valuable knowledge. In APQC's study *Using Communities of Practice to Drive Organizational Performance and Innovation,* we validated this prediction and identified several critical success factors for designing communities. We found that, among the benchmarked best-practice organizations, communities of practice are viewed as an essential practice that improve time to market, response time, employee development, organizational learning, and change implementation.

In 2009, we benchmarked how organizations sustain communities and ensure that they are deeply integrated into their respective organization's cultures. Some of the most robust communities are global. This is the case in ConocoPhillips, Fluor, and Schumberger, among many others. Their examples follow.

- *ConocoPhillips.* Although communities of practice have existed informally for more than 20 years at ConocoPhillips, the first formalized networks of excellence emerged in 2004. Today, there are more than 120 networks aligned with business functions. Portals are open and global, and both contract and full-time employees have access to most network activity. An organization-wide knowledge-sharing team oversees network activities. This team is supported by a team of leaders from different divisions and functional areas around the globe. The leadership team helps set direction and strategy for the networks.

- *Fluor.* Communities serve as a means to maintain and enhance technical excellence, set and maintain standards, and provide professional adoption of those standards by members at Fluor. Communities of practice also help Fluor determine when to consolidate or retire practices, which results in standardized global practices across the organization. Today, Fluor maintains 46 established communities encompassing 24,000 active community members dispersed globally. Virtually all of Fluor's professional employees participate in communities, including more than 3,500 subject matter experts in more than 1,000 areas. There is a high volume of ongoing community activity, including more than 10,000 searches per day, 2,600 attachment views or downloads per day, and 10,000 forum reads per week.

- *Schlumberger.* In 1998, Schlumberger began its Eureka communities with the launch of 12 core communities focused on technical knowledge areas that were critical to the organization. There are now 157 communities covering a variety of operational and functional areas. The purpose of Eureka communities is to provide technical input across the organization, as well as to help members learn and engage in problem solving around specific issues.

    Schlumberger held its first election for community leaders in 2000, and this electoral system has proven to be highly successful. Today, 339 elected leaders manage Schlumberger's communities, which boast 23,000 members worldwide from field operations, engineering, research, and manufacturing. Community membership includes new hires as well as senior managers and subject matter experts. Communities vary in size; some have more than 4,000 members, whereas others have fewer than 500.

Among these best-practice organizations and others, we've seen a number of similar characteristics. For example, such organizations connect employees across regions and have formal approaches to support and sustain their community environments. Consistency of KM leadership is also a prevalent theme and an advantage. Leadership of KM and community efforts has been stable at ConocoPhillips and Fluor almost from the beginning of its community strategy. Also, best-practice organizations have resource structures that support the communities. Finally, among best-practice organizations, communities exist to fulfill a need or objective. They rely on communities to solve problems, identify best practices, develop solutions, and prevent failures. Organizations such as these often create sublevel communities or special interest communities within the larger communities. Organizational objectives clearly link to community activities, and performance measures track community output to better communicate that value to stakeholders.

Ten Traits of Successful Communities

1. A compelling, clear value proposition for all involved
2. A dedicated, skilled facilitator or leader
3. A coherent, comprehensive knowledge map for the core content of the community
4. An outlined, easy-to-follow knowledge-sharing process
5. An appropriate technology medium that facilitates knowledge exchange, retrieval, and collaboration
6. Communication and training plans for members and interested stakeholders
7. An up-to-date, dynamic roster of community members
8. Several key metrics of success to show results
9. A recognition plan for participants
10. An agenda of critical topics to cover for the first—and next—three to six months of existence

Now that we've looked at common characteristics, let's examine some unique community practices at these organizations:

- *ConocoPhillips's financial impact process.* Assessing the financial impact of community activity is important at every organization. At ConocoPhillips, impact is tracked in a unique way. When employees submit a network success story, they detail measurable, tangible gains such as cost savings, reduced cycle times, and safety and environmental improvements. Each success story includes a benefits summary that leadership must validate before it is published. A roll-up organizational value report calculates estimated savings from community activities by region so it can show the tangible value provided by networks. ConocoPhillips calculates that in their first four years, communities of practice provided hundreds of millions of dollars in cumulative value.

- *Fluor's protégé program.* Fluor's subject matter expert protégé program stands out as an effective method to mentor and engage future experts while helping support the expert's role in the community. The program pairs entry- and midlevel employees with senior-level experts within a discipline network to better accelerate learning. Subject matter experts get assistance from the more junior employees to do the work of the community: discuss projects and technical areas, develop new knowledge to support a gap in domain knowledge, review existing knowledge procedures, and help answer network forum questions. This approach helps everyone by leveraging the enthusiasm of newer employees and experience of tenured employees within the community space.

- *Schlumberger's community leader election process.* Schlumberger facilitates an annual leader election process, which serves multiple purposes. First, it helps sustain member engagement. Leadership candidates are self-nominated and must be seconded by a community member before they can participate. Leaders campaign on a platform of what they will help the community accomplish and define expected outcomes. The self-nomination process ensures candidates are committed and gives community members a voice and stake in their leadership. Second, the election process increases buy-in and support for time spent on managing communities. Before running in an election, nominees must have their managers approve the time that will be spent managing the community and agree that leadership commitments will be incorporated into the day-to-day responsibilities. Third, the election process is a strong indicator of community health. In healthy communities, members are excited to step up and nominate themselves as potential leaders. By contrast, if a community shows little or no interest in the election process, then this suggests that the community is in trouble.

Community Leadership Matters

Communities and networks will succeed or fail based on the competency of community leaders and their (volunteer) core teams because they are the face of KM to your organization. These community roles should be clearly defined and communicated. ConocoPhillips, for example, uses its network business case to summarize resources and identify individuals to serve in specific roles and also provides community role descriptions and examples online.

From APQC's research, we have compiled the core critical success factors for communities of practice:

- Create a consistent, enterprise approach, and build on established networks where possible.
- Ensure that communities align with organizational needs and fulfill explicit objectives. Distinguish between formal communities and ad hoc, short-term collaborations. Also distinguish communities from do-it-yourself collaboration capabilities built into an IT infrastructure (Microsoft SharePoint, for example). Establish criteria and basic requirements for a formal community. Demonstrate what happens if you open a storefront (a community Web site) without any merchandise (content) or sales clerks (leaders and promoters).
- Secure and then maintain the support of managers, executives, and subject matter experts. Ensure communities are seen as a legitimate way to spend time.
- Focus on connecting employees across organizational lines, regions, and functions.
- Leverage technology thoughtfully. New tools should provide enhanced connectivity and value.
- Clearly articulate the roles and responsibilities of community leaders, and make sure these employees are backed by a distributed network of supporters. Provide content managers and systems, community coordinators, and IT applications. All communities depend on some central resources—

especially at the beginning—for consulting, training, and content management.

- Ensure each community has a coherent, comprehensive knowledge map for its core content, as well as easy-to-follow knowledge-sharing processes.
- Hold communities accountable for producing and stewarding critical knowledge (and possibly for results as well).
- Measure how the communities deliver value to your organization, and find meaningful ways to communicate that value organization-wide. Depending on the objectives of a community, measures may include the investment and resources required to sustain communities, the level of activity, and the degree to which knowledge and practices are transferred.
- Ensure long-term success by removing competing priorities and continuing to align community objectives with ever-changing organizational needs.

The Balance in Communities

Some organizations redefine a community broadly to include everyone who uses a knowledge portal. We agree that good enterprise collaboration tools can rapidly respond to do-it-yourselfers who just need a short-term collaboration capability, perhaps more closely mirroring the constantly shifting nature of project work. On the other hand, not heeding the people, process, and content preparation needed to make a community work could lead to moribund sites and a bad rap for KM. APQC has found that the most effective communities are woven deeply into the fabric of the organization: functionally, by discipline, and by strategic issue. Some organizations have established and positioned a formal, organization-wide Center of Excellence to promote community consistency, health, and economies of scale.

Lessons Learned

Who in a big organization hasn't observed corporate amnesia? KM's antidote is to provide approaches to aid collective memory and capture lessons, experiences, and practices. Sometimes called after-action reviews, project milestone reviews, post-mortems, or event debriefs, these lessons-learned approaches capture knowledge from projects, events, or other work to apply in similar situations. In short, it's all about not repeating mistakes.

A lessons-learned approach typically boils down to a few key questions:

- What was supposed to happen?
- What actually happened?
- Why was there a difference or variation?
- Who else needs to know this information?

The two biggest challenges to any KM approach are getting employees to participate and getting employees to reuse captured knowledge. A good lessons-learned approach should address both of these challenges. By focusing on existing projects or processes, those involved are already engaged and have a vested interest in performing well as a team. The existing project or process also provides a shared experience base, context, and target to reuse lessons across the enterprise.

Lessons-learned approaches can help your organization:

- Avoid redundancy and reinvention, reuse past designs and experiences, and build on lessons.
- Improve the quality of products and services while reducing errors, rework, and cycle times.
- Standardize best practices and, as a result, improve productivity and efficiency and reduce operating costs.
- Enhance learning proficiency and professional development, reduce time to competency, shorten learning curves, and integrate training and learning initiatives.
- Build a knowledge-sharing culture.

Yet, for all their popularity, lessons-learned approaches regularly fail to deliver the intended results. Lessons may be captured, but they are often not absorbed or applied even within the same project, much less elsewhere in an organization. What is so difficult about lessons-learned approaches that make many organizations' efforts wither away?

We've found the following common problems:

- *Context.* If a lesson is captured without the proper context (e.g., description of project, equipment specifications, political environment, and scientific data), then the end users cannot apply it properly to their own projects. Also, lessons are typically rich with experience and situations. The tacit nature of this information sometimes doesn't (or can't) get captured explicitly in a meaningful story. A dialogue is needed to build understanding.

- *Storage and retrieval.* Organizations often have lessons-learned databases or repositories where lessons go to die because they are not tagged properly and therefore cannot be retrieved.
- *Understanding the customer.* Is the customer for the lesson the *current* team that is in the midst of a project, or is the customer a *future* project manager or team working on a similar problem or task? Or both? A clear understanding of the customer for the lesson drives the objectives for a lessons-learned approach, the development of any templates or tools, and the necessary process and impact measures.

In APQC's study *Cutting the Cost of Not Knowing: Lessons Learned Systems People Really Use,* we benchmarked a number of organizations with mature lessons-learned approaches and found common characteristics. The best-practice organizations each followed their own version of the following steps:

- Determine the strategic objectives for the lessons-learned approach.
- Create governance processes and clearly defined roles.
- Design the lessons-learned approach.
- Ensure participation.
- Measure the impact of the lessons-learned approach.

These steps reflect the process you will use again and again in designing KM approaches for your enterprise KM program.

The U.S. Army Center for Army Lessons Learned (CALL) is a first-rate example of an organization that long ago embraced the purpose and benefits of having a defined, formal lessons-learned approach. Within the U.S. Army, the Center for Army Lessons Learned has a mission to collect, analyze, disseminate, integrate, and archive observations, insights, and lessons to support military operations. The Center uses different types of approaches to execute its lessons-learned approach, depending on the context or situation in which the lesson or lessons occur. It also produces numerous publications, designed for different audiences, that are intended to enable the transfer of lessons learned to those who need them.

The Road Less Traveled: Path A or Path B?

From APQC's benchmarking research, we've seen that the strategic imperative can drive a lessons-learned approach to one of two paths, or possibly both. In Path A, you support current process or project teams with a lessons-learned approach built into the project or process methodology, thus enabling participants to adapt and apply their lessons to the current project. In Path B, you foster future reuse by capturing lessons learned during projects or processes and then creating a mechanism by which lessons learned are made available to future projects or employees.

Virtually every organization can benefit from taking Path A. Organizations that repeat similar projects or processes across multiple sites or over time will benefit from Path B, but it is more difficult for the same reason that Path A is easier: The same employees are not the source and the recipient of the lesson, and the context has changed. Ideally, your organization will enable both paths, which each require different processes, people, and investments. The decision will depend on the locus of the problem and the scale of opportunity to reuse the lessons.

For example, within the U.S. Army, the Center for Army Lessons Learned focuses on adapting and applying lessons to current operations (Path A). This is because the most pressing need is to capture lessons learned from soldiers and immediately use those lessons in the current wars. However, a secondary focus involves retaining knowledge for reuse in future, similar situations (Path B). For Path A, lessons learned are designed for rapid capture, vetting, and turnaround of lessons into action. The Center for Army Lessons Learned sends teams to the field and ensures that all results are analyzed. Some of these lessons are retained for Path B—longer-term use—and can become army doctrine. To support that path, a different set of processes and enablers are used.

The U.S. Army Armament Research, Development and Engineering Center (ARDEC) began with a well-established structure for applying lessons to current projects (Path A) and is currently focused on making lessons available organization-wide (Path

B) by encouraging participation and reuse in contexts that are far removed from the original lessons.

With Path A, the primary customer for lessons learned is the team in the middle of a project or the soldier in a battle zone. Why is the value proposition for participants so much higher with this path? The members of a project are highly engaged and in a teachable moment when they identify and learn a lesson. These participants can immediately benefit from identifying and using lessons to improve their current circumstances and chance for success. From a participant perspective, the value of taking part in lessons-learned activities is much clearer than if the teams (or soldiers) were capturing lessons only to improve performance in future projects (or theaters of war). When your organization pursues this path, other divisions or functions are secondary customers for the lessons learned.

The critical design issue for Path A is to capture lessons at key milestones along the way while there is still time for the current project to benefit. Project teams will lose some interest as the project draws to a close and they prepare to move on.

When designing a lessons-learned strategy for Path A, pilot the approach within specific projects for which the benefits of capturing and using lessons will be especially profound. Once the value of the lessons-learned approach is established, then embed lessons-learned events at key milestones in your organization's project management methodology or process. This will increase the likelihood of transfer to other recipients, as well as build early advocates for the lessons-learned approach.

The challenge for path B, on the other hand, is to ensure that the process improvements and lessons are incorporated into future practice and projects. The critical design issue here is that the recipient of a lesson is not the same person or project that identified the lesson. At a minimum, you need to have:

- A clear process for how employees can search for lessons learned
- Encouragement by process owners to use past lessons, which creates motivation and a teachable moment mentality in employees
- A user-friendly repository that provides easy access to employees and lessons

- Neutral facilitators to help bridge the gap between the original context and the new one

You should also consider the issue of lessons-learned transfer when staffing new projects. As employees serve on other projects, they cross-pollinate lessons. Think about staffing strategically to ensure that this bumblebee approach works.[1]

For both paths, your ability to take advantage of past experience is directly proportional to the speed at which you capture that experience and make it available to others.

At ARDEC, employees are able to submit lessons to a library at any time, rather than only at specific junctures. These lessons are reviewed regularly by teams consisting of owners of the lessons-learned process, process owners, and the lesson submitter. The way in which this process is structured ensures that all employees can obtain quick access to lessons.

The Center for Army Lessons Learned takes a tiered approach to improve publishing speed. Simple lessons can be shared electronically with other units, army schools, training centers, and other services within one to seven days. More complex lessons are assessed for gaps in tactics and training and are published within 100 days. Finally, where doctrine may have to be modified, lessons-learned information is provided as needed and is integrated into the doctrine development process.

We've found that the best lessons-learned approaches balance speed with quality. Each published lesson is first reviewed by subject matter experts or process owners so employees can be confident that the lessons they retrieve and reuse are accurate and valuable.

Lessons-Learned Methodology

Regardless of which path you choose, the journey is enhanced immeasurably if you have a widely deployed and mature process improvement or project management methodology. Not every organization will have this advantage, but a process management orientation drives and enhances a lessons-learned approach. A standardized process management approach also increases the likelihood that an improvement resulting from a lesson will transfer easily to other parts of your organization. Less translation has to take place for the lesson to fit into other areas or situations.

Let's close this section with a critical success factor for lessons-learned processes. A key factor is the integration of the lessons-learned process into the standard way work or projects are conducted. Ensure that the capture and reuse of lessons are viewed as critical components of the work flow itself, and employees will be much more inclined to turn to lessons learned for guidance. Employees then know that changes to project management practices, tactics, or doctrine emanate from lessons learned.

Transfer of Best Practices

In *If Only We Knew What We Know,* we shared what was then known about knowledge and best practices transfer. Twelve years later, it's still a great resource when you're ready to take an in-depth look at the transfer of best practices. Since then, our knowledge has continued to grow through research and practice.

The ability to rapidly identify and adopt superior practices remains an important source of competitive advantage. No matter what the industry, reusing successfully demonstrated practices can lead to shorter cycle times, faster ramp-up, higher customer satisfaction, better decisions, reduced risks, and lower costs. During APQC's study *Facilitated Transfer of Best Practices,* we found that organizations effective at transferring best practices rather than reinventing or ignoring them are saving or creating millions of dollars in value.

By sharing what works best in other parts of an organization, employees get theory, evidence, and expertise all in one. It is a lot harder (but, unfortunately, not impossible) to ignore or dispute the value of a practice when it has bottom-line evidence. By embedding the knowledge in action, best practices transfer can help others in your organization learn better, faster, and more effectively.

But the internal transfer of best practices is not as simple as picking up a wiring diagram or process flow chart and faxing it to another location. Like any KM approach, it takes an organized strategy, a clear focus, significant resources, and a way to overcome the enablers and disablers that encourage or impede transfer.

In benchmarking best-practice organizations, we've found some common characteristics of successful transfer approaches:

- There is an explicit and standard transfer process in place.
- The transfer approach is available for use throughout the organization.
- A central group facilitates the transfer approach.
- Designated roles and significant resources are devoted to the transfer approach.
- Transfer or replication is integrated with other improvement initiatives.

We've found three situations in which a transfer approach is appropriate: when the business model entails leveraging a fixed set of resources through cost minimization; when the business model requires a standardized approach in multiple markets; and when cost reduction, quality enhancement, or consistency of customer (or employee) experience is an important driver.

When the business model meets one or more of the aforementioned situations, the decision to invest in systematic transfer programs hinges on the potential return on investment, including that:

- Multiple locations perform similar or identical practices
- A significant number of these practices are relatively stable and do not need frequent transformation to respond to external market changes
- There is reason to believe that either existing practices or optimized practices are superior to others and can be adopted or replicated in many locations
- A measurable and significant financial or strategic return on investment is feasible if processes are standardized or optimized across multiple locations
- Significant resources are available to support the knowledge transfer
- A culture of business unit autonomy is not an overwhelming barrier

Once the business case is clear, it is important to develop a transfer process appropriate to your organization. A systematic and robust transfer process usually includes steps to:

- Identify best practices
- Capture or document tacit and explicit knowledge
- Review, evaluate, or validate the practices

- Communicate and share the practices, possibly including enabling a dialogue or exchange between a potential recipient and the source of the practice
- Provide support to help a recipient adapt or adopt the practices

Let's look at three KM programs that successfully transfer best practices among employees.

1. *Ford Motor Co.* Ford's primary knowledge-sharing process, called best practice replication, began in the mid-1990s as a means to drive productivity improvement across manufacturing sites. It has since branched out to other disciplines in Ford. The key features of Ford's approach are a clear link to the organization's key strategies, a well-defined transfer process, clearly defined roles and responsibilities, and established metrics to measure the financial and operational impact of the replications. Results have exceeded $100 million in value since its inception.
2. *CEMEX, S.A. de C.V.* CEMEX is the largest of producer of cement in the American continents. After significant global expansion in 1985, the organization set out to manage its knowledge base more efficiently, identify and disseminate best practices, standardize processes, implement key technologies, and foster innovation—all through best practices transfer.
3. *Tata Iron and Steel Company, Ltd.* Tata Iron and Steel gives employees stretch goals each year, which encourage them to take advantage of learning opportunities and chances to adopt best practices from others. Transfer occurs in communities of practice. As a result, Tata Iron and Steel has dramatically improved its margins.

Criteria for Transferring Best Practices

APQC developed the following criteria for selecting practices to transfer with a mining company while developing its best practices transfer approach.

- *Value creation.* Would the adoption of this practice create value?
- *Profitability.* Would adoption of this practice be highly profitable?

- *Strategy alignment.* Does this practice align with the corporate strategy?
- *Time in application.* Has this practice been in application a reasonable amount of time?
- *Results measurability.* Can one measure the effects of this practice on process results?
- *Reproducibility.* Is it reproducible?
- *Conceptual base.* Does the practice have a sound conceptual base?
- *Meets unmet need.* Does the practice satisfy a critical unmet need?

An examination of critical success factors is especially important for this approach because knowledge and best practices exist in every organization, yet employees rarely share them. And even when they do share them, practices are not necessarily implemented. As APQC's chairman Jack Grayson often says: "Just because you broadcast something does not mean the receiver is on. And just because the receiver is on does not mean there'll be any action following."

The challenges might involve time, process ambiguity, a lack of incentive, culture, ego, skepticism, or even a lack of awareness of the practices. To address these challenges, some critical success factors follow.

- Consider more than just direct site-to-site transfer between a single source and recipients. You can mediate site-to-site transfer using a core team, experts, or standing communities that identify, validate, and disseminate practices.
- Adapt the approach to your organization. Transfer models vary by how you define, identify, or create best practices; the role of validation through which you deem a practice *best;* whether adoption of the practice is mandatory or voluntary; and the extent of support you provide for adoption.
- Look for opportunities to include best practices transfer within any organization-wide process improvement efforts. In some organizations, there is a convergence of KM tools and principles with rigorous process improvement methodologies, including Six Sigma and process reengineering techniques. The improvement methodology plays a role in defining and codifying the practice, as well as supporting its implementation.

- Secure strong involvement and encouragement from senior leadership, robust change management strategies (especially for mandatory adoption), and extensive resources and staffing to support the transfer itself.
- Prepare for mandatory adoption to require more facilitation and rigor. The costs will be higher than for models allowing voluntary adoption. Mandatory adoption is a characteristic of a process standardization approach.
- You need a defined organizational unit to support the transfer of best practices and enable clearly designated roles and accountability.
- Use outcome measures more often than other KM approaches.

Closing Comments

These long-established KM approaches illustrate how robust KM has become. Much more about these approaches and how to implement them can be found through APQC.

Surrounding these proven KM approaches are the policies, infrastructure, roles, and change management strategies necessary to support them. A robust KM approach should also include the ability to track the activity and to measure its impact. We address these important issues in depth in Chapters 8, 9, and 10.

But KM is not static. What keeps it exciting and fresh are the way KM professionals respond to the cultural forces swirling around us. Approaches emerging out of social computing hold great promise to provide new ways of achieving KM's long-held objectives. Could we address the virtual teachable moment by making employees better at some of the user-controlled tools? Can we make the process of capturing and sharing knowledge easier and more in the flow of work? That is what we explore in Chapter 6.

Implementation Resources

The following APQC resources can help you implement these proven approaches:

- Audio: *Carla O'Dell on the Transfer of Knowledge and Best Practices*
- *Building and Sustaining Communities of Practice*

- *Communities of Practice and Associations: How to Build and Sustain Effective Communities in Your Associations*
- *Communities of Practice: An APQC Overview*
- *Cutting the Cost of Not Knowing: Lessons-Learned Systems People Really Use*
- *Facilitated Transfer of Best Practices*
- *If Only We Knew What We Know: The Transfer of Internal Knowledge and Best Practice*
- *Lessons-Learned Systems People Really Use: Study Overview*
- *Networks: Compete on Knowledge with Communities of Practice*
- *Sustaining Effective Communities of Practice*
- APQC Training: *Building and Sustaining Communities of Practice*
- *Using Communities of Practice to Drive Organizational Performance and Innovation*

These resources—along with APQC's custom advisory services and more than 1,000 articles focused on KM—are available at www.apqc.org and through this book's Web site at www.newedgeinknowledge.com.

Note

1. The bumblebee approach is described in more detail in C. Jackson Grayson and Carla O'Dell, *If Only We Knew What We Know: Transfer of Internal Knowledge and Best Practice* (New York: Free Press, 1998).

CHAPTER 6

Emerging Knowledge Management Approaches

The emerging technologies of Web 2.0 are a significant new frontier for KM. Social computing, with its popular networking and collaborative technologies, is making its way into our organizations as Enterprise 2.0. And related to this user-driven phenomenon are mobile devices. As previewed in Chapter 1, these trends have significant implications for KM.

Web 2.0 refers to technologies such as social networking sites, blogs and microblogs, wikis, social tagging, social bookmarking, mashups, and virtual spaces. *Social computing* refers to the new relationships and power structures that result (Li, Charron, and Favier 2006). *Enterprise 2.0* refers to the use of social computing in a business environment. Unlike centrally managed corporate IT applications, these tools are easy to use, user-controlled, low or no cost, and spontaneous and self-organizing.

Is there anything we can learn from these technologies—which we refer to going forward simply as 2.0 tools—that will help us create intimacy across large distances and promote knowledge sharing among coworkers? This chapter looks at the implications of 2.0 tools for KM, with Chapter 7 entirely focused on the unique and important social networking aspect.

2.0 Tools

Blogs. Short for *Web logs,* these are online journals or diaries.

Collaboration tools (synchronous and asynchronous). Not strictly Web 2.0 tools, collaboration tools include a wide range of applications that enable teams and communities to work together. Microsoft SharePoint is a widely used example.

Expertise location. This is an integrated approach involving people, processes, technology, and content that is designed to link people to information about others, identify people with expertise and link them to those with questions or problems, and identify participants for projects requiring specific expertise.

Mashup. This is a combination of two media sources to create a new content source.

Microblog. Short blog broadcasts. Microblogs such as Twitter publish succinct content such as status updates in a one-to-many format.

Podcasts. These audio and video digital media files can be downloaded onto computers and mobile devices.

RSS (Really Simple Syndication). RSS allows people to subscribe to online sources of news, blogs, podcasts, and so forth, and receive alerts. It provides the ability to aggregate sources into one location. We consider it a 2.0 tool because it fits well with delivery to mobile devices.

Social bookmarking, folksonomies, and collaborative tagging. Social bookmarking is an online, user-defined taxonomy system for bookmarks. When applied to individual content items, such taxonomy is sometimes called a folksonomy, and the bookmarks are referred to as tags. Tagging may also refer to the metatags applied by users, or automatically generated into tag clouds.

Social networking. This refers to systems that allow members of a specific site to learn about other members' skills, talents, knowledge, and preferences.

Virtual spaces. Virtual spaces simulate reality and help users interact and retrieve information virtually.

Wikis. These are systems for collaborative content sharing, editing, and publishing. Wikis allow many authors to contribute to an online document or discussion; they also enable the coordination of teams and projects through a shared online space.

The Promise of Social Computing

When it comes to using social computing at work, the reality has yet to catch up with the hype and the hope. Adoption has been much slower to date than advocates would like. Although some organizations such as IBM Global Business Services and MITRE have rebuilt their entire KM programs and IT infrastructures to capitalize on this new functionality, they are the exception. The majority of KM programs use a wiki here and there, leaving their marketing, public relations, and customer-facing Web teams to take the lead with new social media tools (Bernoff and Li 2008).[1] Many successful KM programs barely use this technology and don't feel like they are missing much.

But there are opportunities for you to consider. In APQC's study *The Role of Evolving Technologies,* we benchmarked how leading organizations adapt these tools to serve their KM strategies. We saw how organizations leverage such tools to accelerate collaboration, facilitate knowledge transfer, and prepare for the future. We were impressed to see how they made these approaches both productive and scalable. Employees were not only contributing content but also creating new content by interacting with one another, and their connections were visible to others, leading to a broader and more democratic sweep of information and involvement. We also found that as use increased, the benefits of social computing multiplied for these organizations.

Social computing promises to democratize relationships and content and the dialectic between authoritative content and prevailing perspectives (i.e., what author James Surowiecki calls the *wisdom of crowds* [2005]). Employees are now determining subject matter expertise and identifying experts by who they go to for help and whose content they read or rate highly. And the digital capability to connect employees is blurring the concepts of *collaboration* and *communities of practice.* As a result, KM is increasingly focused on connecting employees and less so on collecting and managing content. (This ability to connect employees can also lead to more and better content.)

Most importantly, 2.0 tools have the potential to address many of the problems that have bedeviled KM applications over the years. Social computing provides the opportunity to:

- Link employees with similar interests and knowledge, including experts and friends
- Decrease the time required to publish content
- Increase the number of publishers and consumers of knowledge within organizations
- Access user-driven content, which means that organizations are less dependent on content managers to generate

knowledge (although such managers are still needed to repackage and repurpose content for other uses)
- Reduce the need for complex taxonomy structures
- Elevate relevant and useful content and sources based on feedback
- Reduce the barriers to entry (because many Web 2.0 tools are open source, inexpensive, and simple to deploy and use)
- Give employees more control over the tools, how they are used, and the content they provide
- Offer knowledge-sharing technologies that are more fun to use than enterprise applications

Yet, except for the last item, these potentials are true for a lot of good communication and collaboration software. So why all the breathless boosterism that characterizes 2.0 tools? The answer is one word: Facebook. With hundreds of millions of users around the world and growth at a blistering pace, it caught everyone's attention. Following fast on its heels is Twitter, which proved its worth in the political riots in Iran. Like most people, we are not as interested in the software as we are in how people can use it to share, collaborate, and make their work more efficient. When people talk about Facebook, they don't talk about the software; they talk about what they are doing with their family and friends. This is how your employees ought to consider social computing tools at work.

Revealing New Facets of Information

When KM first appeared on the scene, it transformed the way we look at work. With KM, we now have the paradigm and perspective to *see* knowledge flows and understand the power that could come from encouraging knowledge assets to flow in new ways.

In the same way, 2.0 tools have shed a new light on the previously hidden social considerations and how that power can be harnessed to create new, actionable knowledge. Consider the multifaceted nature of information:

- *The information itself.* The content or the message.
- *The information about the information.* Author, date, and a variety of metadata and tags that add context to the information, especially the tags employees add as they use the information.

- *The information that the information exists.* Awareness through search results, alerts, and RSS feeds, ideal for mobile devices.
- *The social facet of information.* Employees' opinions about the content, as well as cross-references and recommendations.

Moreover, social computing provides a forum for technologically adventurous employees to experiment with collaborative tools and give the KM group information about what might work for the organization at large. These 2.0 tools can enable organizations to track what employees are doing online and with whom and, in doing so, generate new information based on patterns of behavior. (The privacy alarms this raises are addressed by allowing employees to opt in to this service.)

With this information, we can analyze activities such as tagging, bookmarking, rating, recommending, commenting, editing, viewing, downloading, and forwarding to improve the employee experience and content accessibility, determine what information is most valuable, and see who is connected to whom. These valuable breadcrumbs dropped by employees as they work allow us to create better paths to the few pieces of content employees really need for a particular task, without disturbing the flow of their work.

The New Generation of Self-Service: The Digital Hub

Chapter 4 discusses the idea of KM *self-service:* technology-enabled access to codified and explicit knowledge. Tools such as portals, search engines, directories, and databases are the traditional stuff of KM self-service. Portals have come a long way, performing as personalized hubs; directories are now supplemented with network connections; and disparate databases can be searched with one query.

What is now emerging is a picture of the ideal self-service vehicle to ensure that employees can easily access knowledge assets at a teachable moment. We call it the *digital hub.* A digital KM hub provides your employees with an electronic, single point of entry to knowledge assets, collaborative work environments, and expertise location from any location, at any time, using any electronic communications device. Through a 24/7 hub, your employees can access needed knowledge, collaborate with colleagues, and connect to experts at their time of need.

Furthermore, a digital KM hub provides an electronic publishing medium for explicit knowledge, a collaborative environment for conducting work or developing ideas, and a marketplace to connect knowledge seekers and providers. An ideal digital KM hub has the following seven best-practice characteristics:

1. Employees have access to documents, exchanges, or expertise when they have a question or need for information or input.
2. There is a set of processes and a technology that can search for relevant employees or documented information in response to a query.
3. The technology enablers are always on, anytime, anyplace, returning results from any database, expertise location, social network analysis, and degrees of separation.
4. The approach is scalable, even globally.
5. Any technical enablers are unobtrusive and available when needed.
6. A system anticipates employee needs based on the work context (e.g., engaged in an engineering project) or role (e.g., project leader or executive).
7. The approach both supports and benefits from a culture of openness to teaching and learning from others during daily work.

The digital hub becomes possible with 2.0 tools. Given these new technologies, KM has even more ways to support the teachable moment in the flow of work.

The Digital Hub at Work

So, where do you start? Let's look at how organizations use some of the most popular 2.0 tools to help employees find content at the teachable moment. (At the end of this chapter, we have short summaries of the Enterprise 2.0 approaches taken by several organizations referred to throughout the following sections.)

Wikis: The Chameleons of Enterprise 2.0

Among members of APQC's KM community, wikis are consistently listed among the most important 2.0 tools for creating new content from a variety of people. Perhaps the familiarity of wikis, due in part to Wikipedia, has led to their popularity. Its markup language is widely known, and it is a free and open-source tool. A wiki is also highly visible and easy to explain, which is critical for widespread use. Employees create content and interact with content created by others, which creates new knowledge in the process. And organizations can kick-start their use by populating the application. The more it is used, the better it gets.

Even organizations with no need for other social computing tools, like Rockwell Collins Inc., find wiki technology useful for content that needs multiple inputs and should be updated frequently. Its uses include collaborative development of procedures and manuals, the creation of FAQ-like databases and glossaries, and posting project information such as meeting minutes and product documentation.

Rockwell Collins took many disparate engineering knowledge stores and combined them inside of a wiki or forum environment. Engineers can now navigate to whatever information they might need, including process flow, training, guidelines, communities of practice, and external sources. The wiki is embedded inside a process tool, which also includes a support forum so that an employee can ask a question, search for relevant articles, or get direct support from subject matter experts.

Siemens AG uses wikis for a variety of projects and purposes: meeting minutes, agendas, product documentation, glossaries, and reports. Typical use scenarios for wikis at Siemens consequently range from a wiki for small workgroups to wikis being used within a Siemens business unit to cross-business wikis. In fact, approximately 60 different wikis reside within Siemens on various platforms.

Additional organizational examples further illustrate its wide applications. Accenture adopted a wiki interface to let users create divergent extensions of a single problem or solution. The result is a vine-like collection of competing ideas to solve ongoing issues. The U.S. Department of State created a wiki for organizational knowledge and decentralized writing and editing; any employee can create and edit articles with proper attribution. The U.S. intelligence community, with leadership from the CIA, created Intellipedia after September 11th to connect disparate sources of intelligence information (CIA 2009a). Hewlett-Packard Company's wiki also supports mass collaboration and acts as a group knowledge base. And Royal

Dutch/Shell Group's wiki is an extremely detailed encyclopedia of the organization, with aggregated knowledge from many existing sources, including training programs.

Wikis, however, are not exempt from challenges. Employees need time to contribute to wikis, but the experts and leaders needed may have the least time to do so. Also, experts—and others—may resent their contributions being edited by strangers or those less experienced than themselves. And collective wisdom may not be wise enough to catch all mistakes. (History tells us that crowds are capable of groupthink and mistakes at least as often as they are wise.)

Blogs

Blogs are the most personal and idiosyncratic of the 2.0 tools. Easily hosted from a variety of sources using all of the commonly available Internet browsers, blogs are the epitomes of personal publishing. The potential to interact and get feedback from others may be blogging's greatest asset, making it both an ad hoc social networking tool (if people comment on your blog) and an application to showcase expertise.

Many organizations' PR departments leverage blogs to publicize the thoughts and ideas of senior leaders, thus providing greater access to executives. Blogs are used by senior managers as communication tools when they need to make announcements (and would like to get employee reactions), to collaborate, and to let specialists spread their knowhow.

But what about useful applications for KM?

Blogging at Royal Dutch/Shell is mainstream, with approximately 415 internal bloggers. One KM application is in its laboratories, where blogs are replacing laboratory notebooks for researchers. Patent offices now accept blogs as an electronic note-taking format, and therefore more senior researchers have begun blogging to document their research. This important change resulted from the discovery among Royal Dutch/Shell's scientists that blogs could capture what had already been done as opposed to what was planned. This started to change the blogging environment because other scientists and researchers began providing additional guidance and comments. Obviously, increased networking among researchers is a good thing.

We found another useful application of blogging at the U.S. Department of State. Ambassadors and diplomats can read each other's blogs or sign on to Web chats to interact with department leaders around the world. Web chats and blogs often help the agency gain a better understanding of regions of interest.

One particular blog at the State Department is run by economic officers in Istanbul, Turkey. It has replaced e-mail to disseminate knowledge on the Turkish economy. The State Department uses blogs as opposed to e-mail because blogs can be properly archived and become part of its departmental record.

Another successful blog at the State Department is for system administrators to share knowledge on IT. The blog is run by IT specialists on four continents. It is primarily a knowledge clearinghouse and discussion forum for systems technologies.

Having seen these useful applications of blogging, we still believe its primary value for internal KM is as a personal publishing outlet for executives, experts, and other employees with something useful to say to a large number of people and to invite their comments.

Social Tagging and Bookmarking

By revealing two of the often hidden facets of information—the information that the information exists and the social facet of information—social computing allows employees to help one another sort through the numerous competing sources and find just what interests them based on what also interests others.

Social tagging and bookmarking allow employees to share links to sites and content they find useful. Employees are able to hone in on sources that others have vetted. Social bookmarks and tags also provide access to links and information that have been highly rated by experts or others in an employee's peer group and enhance the ability of search engines to return items of relevance and value.

These systems have several advantages over traditional automated search and classification software. Social bookmarking and tag-based classification of online resources is done by human beings, who understand the content and context, as opposed to software that algorithmically attempts to determine the meaning of a resource by keywords. Additionally, resources that are of more use are bookmarked by more employees. Thus, such a system will rank a resource based on its perceived utility. This is arguably more useful than a ranking based on the number of external links pointing to it.

MITRE uses Onomi, an internal tool from Web service delicious, to share and manage personal bookmarks. Bookmarks can be edited, deleted, e-mailed, or searched. Employees can view which bookmarks are accessed most frequently and can retrieve shared bookmarks by looking at individuals' profiles. When an employee hovers a cursor over an individual's name, the system displays the number of bookmarks submitted by that individual as well as a phone number at which that individual can be reached in case the employee needs additional information. Employees can also tag bookmarks and incorporate RSS feeds that notify them when a new bookmark is added by a particular individual.

Social tagging is integrated into IBM Global Business Services' federated search function, and employees are able to filter search results by social tags. Tag data are also used for social network–based content recommendation services and leveraged to provide a person-centered view of content. Employees are able to view the names of individuals who have tagged certain sites; they can also search by an individual to view what that person has tagged. A watch list can be created to track what a particular expert or colleague tags on a daily basis. From a KM perspective, this virtual apprenticeship is a nice benefit of social tagging and RSS feeds.

Ratings and Recommendations

Like tagging, ratings thrive when enough employees participate. The most familiar example of a rating system is the Amazon.com customer reviews and ratings system. Customer ratings help sort through the mass of products by promoting the most relevant and, perhaps, lesser-known items.

Accenture uses a tool that adopts a user-rating approach, much like other mass collaborative applications such as YouTube. Through this tool, employees can rate others' ideas, and the best (or most popular) ideas rise to the top for management review. In one example, the tool was used to generate ideas to help a client improve its customers' experience. Users of the tool were given some on-boarding guidance to help them feel qualified to contribute ideas. This particular implementation was used by more than 300 people, and 75 customer service improvement ideas surfaced.

In the past, a repository housing 150,000 content items would have been viewed as unmanageable. Today, thanks to integrated searches and a rating system, IBM Global Business Services employees are able to quickly identify the best and most reusable content. The organization's rating system helps employees locate high-quality documents while filtering out materials that may not be useful or relevant. Using simple browser plug-ins that pop up on their desktops, employees can rate documents on a 1 to 5 scale. Employees can also attach comments to documents, which are immediately available to other employees. Ratings are compiled in a central database and are compared to other ratings to produce an average quality rating for each document. Content ratings are factored into search and indexing results, which ultimately serve to highlight the collective wisdom of the organization.

We do offer the caution, however, that employees may not feel comfortable rating their colleagues' content. Unlike Amazon, the rating is not anonymous and could influence relationships. But if an employee shares a niche interest with someone, then that rating will mean as much or more than the collective average.

Federated Search Functions

Everyone laments information overload. Running separate searches on separate sites is also a pain. Employees want integrated search results to relevant resources, experts, and communities. They expect immediate access to the people and content they need to do their jobs.

Why have employees historically disliked internal search engines? *Findability.* Content is not tagged correctly or is hidden in a variety of local databases. That's where federated search functions and the power of mining all the facets of information really shine. *Federated search* refers to technology that searches across multiple databases and uses criteria other than simple frequency of occurrence to rate the relevancy of an item. This technology allows a search engine to use social tags, bookmarks, and ratings to elevate content from a variety of sources.

Integrated search is a key component of MITRE's 2.0 platform. Through *Moogle* (MITRE's version of Google), all employees have access to general content, expertise location, and lists of people in forums and SharePoint sites. Every employee is permitted to view community sites; its search function draws from this knowledge base for its integrated searches.

Enhancing accessibility to content was one of Royal Dutch/ Shell's reasons for a corporate wiki with a federated search function. The need to facilitate prompt access to critical information was the impetus behind the creation of its wiki application. Although employees can add and edit the information in Shell Wiki, only 20 percent of the wiki's current content was provided by wiki users; the other 80 percent represents content that was already available in the organization. These materials were loaded into Shell Wiki to improve distribution and ensure that employees could access relevant information quickly and efficiently.

Using Accenture's federated search function, its employees can either search a broad range of knowledge assets from a single point of access or search deeply within an attachment. Content from the top 50 Accenture content applications (corporate content, knowledge, training, methodologies, experts, discussions, and external content) are searchable in one integrated, easy-to-use application.

RSS

Really Simple Syndication (RSS) allows employees to subscribe to alerts that content has been updated or added to internal and external sites, including project sites, databases, and blogs. Furthermore, when employees want to know more, a simple click can take them to the alerting content. Equally as significant, they can choose to ignore it. RSS has quickly become a powerful means to disseminate all kinds of information, which helps employees control the content they receive.

Organizations use these feeds for tutorials, streaming audio lectures, PDF proposals, PowerPoint presentations, podcasts of sales meetings, and advertising portfolios, among more traditional uses. RSS can quickly become a go-to tool for access to the most up-to-date information. With the advent of having links, photos, and other useful media included in the alert, the possibilities for knowledge sharing are increasing. RSS is particularly suited to mobile devices, where an alert may be the most an employee wants to know when they are on the go.

As a complement to MITRE's other KM approaches, its social tagging and bookmarking tool allows users to share both internal and external resources, thus increasing the number of access points to content. Users can see who is interested in the same topics—thanks to integration with an online phone book—and receive RSS feeds for every feature (e.g., what a particular organization is posting, bookmarks by topic).

Microblogs

Instant messaging (IM) and e-mail are no longer the only go-to sources for quick communication or to find out where or what a colleague is working on. Microblogging is simple and, thanks to Twitter, popular. We define microblogging as the act of communicating one-to-many by short message. The communication may include photos, audio clips, or links to other content. Whereas IM is private and usually lost, microblogging is now a matter of public record.

Tweets for the Ages

In April 2010, Twitter gifted the U.S. Library of Congress with its entire archive of public Twitter feeds. According to the library's official blog (http://blogs.loc.gov/loc/2010/04/the-library-and-twitter-an-faq/), tweets have the same cultural significance as the first telegram:

> Twitter is part of the historical record of communication, news reporting, and social trends—all of which complement the Library's existing cultural heritage collections. It is a direct record of important events such as the 2008 U.S. presidential election or the "Green Revolution" in Iran. . . . Individually, tweets might seem insignificant, but viewed in the aggregate, they can be a resource for future generations to understand life in the 21st century.

Microblogging provides a sense of what employees are up to without requiring followers to respond unless they want to. This means employees can step in and out of the flow of information as it suits them, and it never queues up with increasing demand of their attention as it does in e-mail. Additionally, employees are in control of whose updates they receive, when they receive them, and on what device.

Microblogging is perfect for mobile employees and mobile devices. Microblogs have just enough information to alert someone to your presence or location, which is very helpful in organizations like MITRE and IBM, where employees are usually not in the office. The ability to "follow" someone allows team leaders and executives to let staff know where they are and what they are working on. From the teachable moment perspective, microblogging is a powerful tool for getting feedback, asking for help, or alerting others to a project or activity that they may find interesting. In addition, microblogging potentially opens up more answers to a query, more connections with others, and more discoveries by both the sender and the receiver.

Employees don't control who follows their posts, although the followers can be counted and in some cases identified. Microblogging can become an accelerator to transparency ("What are you doing?"), improved communications, and situational awareness (people know where you are). However, it may not directly contribute to explicit content that can be housed in your organization's knowledge base. It serves more as a breeze of information passing through and then gone. (However, you can make microblogs searchable and permanent.)

MITRE developed TWITRE (from Twitter's existing code) as a solution for common problems such as skills finding, staff location awareness, and availability. TWITRE allows employees to share and post meeting events on their calendars, as well as use presence indicators already available through the Microsoft Office suite to communicate availability. Its microblogging capabilities allow employees to sidestep the drawbacks of traditional calendars (i.e., too focused on meetings, too much or too little information shared, and not up to date) to provide a real-time stream of location and status. The TWITRE tool encompasses a desktop view of a contact's location and availability, an alert system for certain keywords, a phone-based expertise finder that is helpful for people outside the MITRE firewall, and large touch-screens in common areas for a public view of the system. The information is populated by employees' inputs, Twitter feeds, and integration with MITRE's time-reporting system.

In a novel case of location-based networking, employees can even press a thumbprint reader next to a public touch screen to indicate when they are in an office's common space. MITRE found that, in addition to leveraging existing connections, the tool fosters new connections among employees. Its pilot public touch screen is the new water cooler space for socializing.

Mobile Devices

Teachable moments often occur when employees are away from the office, working with a client, or in the field. And a growing number of employees operate entirely remotely. Mobile devices enable organizations to respond to employees' teachable moments, no matter when or where they occur. Employees can access information as needed with little-to-no wait time, using less support and funding than traditional desktop computing.

We believe the majority of KM professionals have not yet addressed the issues presented by mobile devices (e.g., Do most of the documents you feed employees fit on a little screen? And what is accessible outside your corporate firewall?). But more and more, mobile device use is making people rethink everything from the use of graphics on Web pages to the appropriate length for e-mail subject lines. The current generation of devices is probably best suited to simple messages such as alerting employees that information exists and where to find it. (Hence, the value of RSS alerts.) If you can get it on a sticky note and it's meaningful and it causes somebody to do something, then you've probably done the right thing. We recommend using mobile devices as a conduit for knowledge capture and flow—not for deep content, but instead for alerts, IM, e-mail, and presence notification.

The growth in types of devices underlines the need to design KM approaches that are agnostic to technology type and vendor. Technology changes rapidly. We recommend designing for employees while making some assumptions about the capabilities of most devices and then designing policies and approaches independent of the device. You may also consider putting preconfigured links on mobile devices' home screens to keep knowledge sharing at the top of your mind.

At IBM Global Business Services, the users of mobile devices are mostly consultants and application management professionals. Employees receive succinct notifications communicating changes such as the presence of new or updated content, based on the subscriber's preferences. By providing notifications, IBM is able to address security issues in that the employee has to go to a secure environment (behind the firewall) to actually view the content.

Conducive Workspaces

There is still knowledge work that doesn't fit on a sticky note and can't be accomplished through Twitter. For tasks that require sustained concentration and critical thinking, KM professionals must find ways to ensure that employees have adequate psychological, virtual, and physical spaces in which to contemplate, reflect, and make decisions. Employees often leave the office to get work done. Thanks to laptops, Wi-Fi, and mobile devices, more employees are choosing to do their deep thinking away from the hubbub of cubicles and coworkers. As long as employees have the willpower to ignore e-mail and turn off their alerts for a period of time while working virtually, it is still possible to find a workspace conducive to solitary critical thinking. The downside is that, by going home to work, employees are running away from face-to-face interaction, which is where so much tacit knowledge is created and shared.

Challenges and Change Management

Many 2.0 tools are easy to use and are familiar. When the business solution looks just like the consumer solution, you don't have to train employees. Although training is less necessary, don't dismiss change management outright.

Social computing works when enough people participate. Online, hundreds of millions of people could contribute to a wiki or rating system. Millions of people now have the experience of publishing to the world. But it is still a small percentage of those who go online. Will 2.0 tools work inside your organization, when only hundreds or thousands of employees might engage?

We believe the answer is a qualified yes—if you employ change management methods to encourage adoption and participation. Employees need encouragement and a rationale for changing the way they work. It is no different for social computing. You still need executive role models, an effective communication plan, clearly defined roles, and recognition when appropriate.

Let's examine some of the challenges and change management issues in detail.

People Are Busy

The KM challenges are still the same when it comes to the use of time. Even among best-practice organizations, 2.0 tools must prove their value in employees' eyes. That is, if employees don't feel that they have time to learn the new applications or if the benefits of the tools aren't perceived to exceed the value of the time spent to learn and use them, then adoption rates suffer. In Chapter 9, we discuss the need for structured communication and marketing to encourage employees to try the tools.

Avoid taking employees out of the work flow to use 2.0 tools. They do want to share and help, if we make it easy for them.

Is This for Work or for Fun?

In *The Economist,* Martin Giles writes: "An astonishing amount of time is being wasted on investigating the amount of time being wasted on social networks. Studies regularly claim that the use of Twitter, Facebook, and other such services poses a threat to corporate wealth. . . . This assumes that people would actually work rather than find some other way to pass the time they have to spare. In the same vein, perhaps companies should also ban water coolers and prohibit people sending e-mails to their friends" (2010).

Trust Is Not Spontaneous

Even early adopters, and especially those operating globally, may have employees who feel uncomfortable sharing in an open forum. Discussion forums have been around in a variety of forms for many years, but now the discussions have moved out of the community space, which many consider to be a comfort zone, to blogs and other organization-wide forums. This opens the contributor to a wider audience and increases the sense of vulnerability for some. Although the whole notion of the wisdom of crowds decreases the fear of sharing for some due to the self-policing aspect, for others it acts as a deterrent. This is especially apparent in organizations that don't promote an "ask first" culture. And some regional cultures, particularly in Asia, may inhibit peer-to-peer sharing.

To promote a cultural shift in thinking, the U.S. Department of State gradually transformed its attitude toward information sharing from "need to know" to "need to share." This, along with a change in the department's operating manual that explicitly promotes the use of blogs and wikis, helped reshape the culture and promote knowledge sharing. The State Department also encourages grass-roots evolution of some of its collaborative technologies.

In a similar vein is the tension between sharing knowledge and information and protecting proprietary content, such as intellectual property. Hewlett-Packard and the State Department both noted to APQC that some of their employees continue to worry about sharing in wikis and blogs where control over who has access to the information and knowledge shared is somewhat tenuous, even if those tools reside inside organizational firewalls.

Risk Management Must Continue

On that note, the organizations APQC has benchmarked have not found internal abuse to be a problem with 2.0 tools. They rely on existing business ethics, e-mail, and communication conduct policies for social computing. They do lightly monitor the use of collaborative 2.0 tools and applications to ensure they are used appropriately. But they primarily rely on topic owners and content moderators to monitor content. The expectation for well-mannered behavior is also enforced through self-policing to quickly address any issues.

Accenture, for example, sets clear expectations regarding collaboration among employees and provides guidance documents that must be reviewed and accepted before an employee uses an application.

And Royal Dutch/Shell relies on mechanisms for quality assurance in forums such as the wiki, with which an expert can be alerted to new content entries and therefore monitor the new content for accuracy and overall quality.

Rockwell Collins has had policies and procedures in place regarding data privacy and security for several years. However, with its move to the use of 2.0 tools, the organization performed additional due diligence. It conducted extensive research on the legal compliance issues related to the use of social media application and created social media use guidelines and FAQs for all employees.

Although issues from intentional misuse haven't been a problem for these best-practice organizations, there are still other risk management concerns when adopting 2.0 tools. We suggest:

- Determining the need and methods for safely migrating legacy content into 2.0 tools

- Governance, since central control of content is no longer a requirement
- Assessing risk for each business function and then for the organization as a whole
- Considering how issues may differ by cultures

Tools Are Not the Answer

We love 2.0 tools but are realists about the notion of viral adoption. Don't make the same old mistake by thinking technology will be a standalone solution automatically embraced by your employees. Without people, processes, and strategic drivers, technologies are abandoned right and left. Usually, they are not even adopted except by the disappointed evangelists.

Open collaboration and idea sharing are great goals, but that doesn't mean there is latent demand among your workforce for the tools that enable them. Is there a perceived problem your chosen approach will help fill? If so, then the approach may spread virally as employees recommend it to others. If this approach does not address an organizational need validated through your KM strategy, then it is going to take a lot of advertising to convince employees they need this new way to communicate or collaborate.

We still believe that communication campaigns will greatly aid adoption, assuming the knowledge value proposition is there to begin with. We also have found the challenges tend to be cultural, not technical: providing time to submit or access knowledge assets, the development of trust among employees, and the perceived value by employees of the tools. (We discuss these in more depth in Chapter 8.)

The best-practice distinction is authorizing the experimental use of applications, encouraging grassroots evolution, and targeting early adopters as champions. Selectively deploying pilots and choosing technically fluent employees to manage them can make your initial rollouts a success. As those successes are publicized, the pull created from them will develop sufficient demand to justify the business case to expand into other areas.

Like many organizations, MITRE struggles to find the right balance between the "let a thousand flowers bloom" approach and a more streamlined, process-oriented attitude toward 2.0 tools. Currently, almost any group or team can pilot a social networking tool; there is no formal gate to approve a pilot. This approach is strategic; the KM group finds that this is an effective way to find out what is important to its employees.

Likewise, the general approach at Royal Dutch/Shell is to support all efforts at an early stage. If employees have an idea and it does not directly violate the strategy or ethics of the organization, then it is generally given time to develop and take root. The goal is to let each community thrive and grow in a way that makes sense for its particular mission and purpose.

But Simplicity Helps

Social computing tools must be easy to use, provide the lowest possible threshold, and require little or no training.

Although IBM Global Business Services occasionally releases three-minute videos to provide guidance on certain social computing tasks (such as how to apply social bookmarking tags), most employees do not require any training to use its practitioner portal. The videos are more to encourage use and raise awareness.

Simplicity in design is important, but so is ease of contribution. IBM Global Business Services uses a basic content submission form with three fields and relies on autotagging. Similarly, MITRE prepopulates as many fields as possible and integrates information across various applications to simplify its data submission process. At Royal Dutch/Shell, much of the content from its learning and development efforts is cut and pasted into Shell Wiki.

Distance Matters More than Age

None of the best-practice organizations we have benchmarked reported problems related to age or generational differences in the use of 2.0 tools. In other words, no generation is more or less likely to use workplace 2.0 tools than any other.

Instead, the more virtual the employee base, the more likely employees will appreciate and support tools that enhance social networking and expert identification. At Royal Dutch/Shell, where employees must interact across the globe, virtual collaboration is a necessity. The organization's Global Connect Web site houses a variety of popular tools that enable and promote virtual collaboration. At MITRE, employees can log in to team rooms from home, and many team meetings are conducted virtually. Even key events such as technical exchange meetings are conducted virtually. Employees at IBM Global Business Services are also scattered across the globe, and 2.0 tools are the starting points for all employee connections.

The size of the audience also matters with 2.0 tool deployment; the larger the total user base, the more likely it is that content will be provided and requests will be fulfilled promptly and effectively. At IBM Global Business Services, MITRE, and Royal Dutch/Shell, social computing tools are effective because they are widely adopted and used. Their organizational cultures are conducive to knowledge sharing; each has had a KM strategy in place for more than 10 years. Their 2.0 tools helped improve existing platforms and provided a more intuitive way to share.

A case can be made that, if knowledge sharing is engrained in your organization, adoption of 2.0 tools may be easier—unless, of course, the existing tools are good enough. If your KM program is new, then it will require a robust KM strategy regardless of tools.

Our Recommendations

Social computing has the potential to make your organization more agile and efficient by improving communication and knowledge sharing. But it may also shift power and the sources of value creation. With innovation moving from a top-down to a bottom-up model, expect a democratization of content creation; anyone can be an author or voice an opinion. And value shifts from expertise to experience, with the locus of control moving from institutions to communities and employees. That is, learning and knowledge creation occur through networks of employees instead of more controlled means of organizational development.

The fears some held that social computing would lead to abuse have not materialized. Instead, consider the emergent risk of such tools becoming so popular out of the mainstream of IT platforms that later corralling the content and the users back into the fold may be difficult. If a social computing tool is ready to be used across your organization, then we recommend having your IT function converge quickly before the user base becomes too large and resistant to change. Otherwise, the content may be expensive to migrate. This can be supported by establishing close ties between the KM program and IT function, especially when determining employee needs and monitoring and supporting early adopters.

Furthermore, finding the perfect tool is not as critical as implementing functional tools quickly, experimenting, and then deciding what to use going forward. The challenge is deciding which among the rapidly changing tools to use, especially given that vendors are continuously adding functions to existing tools. Don't select applications that depend on significant enterprise-level governance, and don't expect employees to be as interested in managing content as they are in connecting to other employees.

Unlike with legacy systems, your organization will not be able to control the speed of technology change. Social media evolution and capability in the personal, consumer world will dictate how well your enterprise version will continue to be accepted. This applies to every social media approach adopted for KM, including mobile devices. Design your content and policies to be as agnostic as possible to device and software; they will change.

And keep in mind that early 2.0 tool adopters have had KM programs in place for years, have extensive experience using enterprise platforms, and are open to experimenting with new tools. IBM Global Business Services, MITRE, and Royal Dutch/Shell each have decade-old KM programs. They can afford to focus on forging relationships instead of aggregating content because their mature KM programs already have a significant amount of content to build on and because the new technologies generate content through employee interactions.

Case Examples

For your reference, short summaries follow of the Enterprise 2.0 approaches taken by several leading organizations referred to throughout this chapter.

Accenture

Accenture uses 2.0 tools to facilitate the evolution of its KM programs and to allow employees to organize and share content as they see fit.

Its Knowledge Exchange houses content to support sales, deliver client work, maintain work histories, capture deliverables and best practices, and connect employees. The application is integrated with its enterprise search engine, collaboration capabilities, and enterprise portal. The Knowledge Exchange also provides access to 400 discussion forums, where employees post questions and view comments of blogs. The Knowledge Exchange also houses 150 communities of practice and the organization's wiki space.

Accenture's portal provides personalized quick links, targeted content based on organization and region, and the ability to subscribe to content areas. Employees are also able to customize the site and incorporate access to key projects.

Accenture People is the organization's primary application to identify and locate employees. Each employee manages a personal workspace, which allows for a full-text search on expertise. Employees create profiles that provide contact information (e.g., e-mail address, telephone number, and location) and brief descriptions of their education, prior work experience, and current projects and roles. Reporting relationships are also listed.

Accenture has also adopted RSS alerts.

Bottom line: Accenture is an excellent example of a centralized digital KM hub that can be used to help an organization compete on the basis of its organizational knowledge.

Hewlett-Packard

Hewlett-Packard uses a portfolio of 2.0 tools including Microsoft SharePoint to support knowledge sharing through communities, portals, virtual rooms, blogs, wikis, podcasts, RSS feeds, and social networking.

The organization supports three different types of communities: role-specific, solution-specific, and specialty forums. In Hewlett-Packard's collaborative team spaces, anyone can create a space. Its intranet primarily enables enterprise searches; it allows employees to track down anyone within the organization. Its intranet is integrated with its KM environment, and the search function is capable of traversing the various KM portals. For expertise location, Hewlett-Packard's KM team relies more heavily on the specialty forums than on other, more formal expertise location tools. And blogging is becoming more popular at Hewlett-Packard; some blogs are focused on particular content, whereas others consist of employees expressing opinions in a more unstructured way. Like blogs, wikis are relatively new at Hewlett-Packard. Wikis are particularly used for mass collaboration and as a group knowledge base. Even internal podcasts help share knowledge assets. And RSS feeds distribute frequently updated content such as blog posts, wiki revisions, forum posts, and knowledge briefs. An internal application called *WaterCooler* allows employees to see a mashup of RSS feeds and also select highlights from desired sources. And finally, Hewlett-Packard uses an internally developed application similar to Facebook for social networking.

Bottom line: Hewlett-Packard seamlessly intertwines 2.0 tools with its traditional KM approaches such as communities of practice.

IBM Global Business Services

IBM Global Business Services uses 2.0 tools to drive new capabilities that enable and support teachable moments. For example, KnowledgeView is IBM's global asset repository, which provides links to methods and reusable assets. The tool is accessible to and popular with employees worldwide. KnowledgeView enables employees to contribute knowledge and offer feedback; it also leverages portlets to push targeted content and links based on employee profiles.

In 2009, IBM Global Business Services began a serious move to 2.0 tools. At the center of this transformation is its practitioner portal, the digital hub for intellectual property, communities, and experts. The portal is a flexible space that can be configured by the employee and provides person-centered views, community-centered views, and organization-centered views. It also offers federated content search functionality, facilitates expertise location, and houses all of the organization's networks and communities. Employee-driven feedback is supplied through tagging, ratings, usage analytics, and content creation and submission. Keeping content current is a key component of the strategy; through the use of autotagging and archiving, IBM Global Business Services is able to make sure that content stays fresh.

IBM Global Business Services also has portlets tailored to employees. Its SmallBlue technology (commercially available as IBM Atlas) looks at what an employee reads and rates highly in order to place appropriate RSS feeds. Employees' own social networks and communities of practice have RSS feeds as well. The objective is to leverage social networking and personal data to create more personalized content pushes.

Bottom line: IBM Global Business Services has catapulted its efforts to be a learning organization to the front of the pack using 2.0 tools.

MITRE

MITRE leverages 2.0 tools to support employees when they experience a teachable moment. Its four primary approaches are its MITRE information Internet, its Moogle search function, community home pages, and its MITREpedia wiki function.

The MITRE information Internet is the primary vehicle for the organization's collaboration and knowledge-sharing efforts. It includes community and team spaces supported by Microsoft SharePoint. From the home page, employees can view corporate headlines and access information on key events. Almost everything on the home page can be customized to align with specific employees' locations or functions. Individual portlets can also be tailored to specific content. A fast jump feature modeled after AOL's keyword search allows employees to access any of 4,000 intuitive and predefined areas.

MITRE's primary search feature, Moogle, is customized and serves as the main organization-wide integration point for federated searches. Through Moogle, employees can also search résumés for experts or project-specific knowledge.

Team members use blogs to summarize brainstorming sessions and meeting notes. Employees can search blogs by title, or they can click on an individual's name to find all blogs posted by that individual. Projects often include question-and-answer blogs to communicate project information.

Onomi, an internal tool from Web service delicious, enables employees to manage and share bookmarks. Bookmarks can be edited, deleted, e-mailed, or searched. By looking at individual profiles, employees can see shared bookmarks and view those bookmarks accessed most frequently.

MITREpedia is MITRE's corporate wiki and information platform, which provides access to people, projects, organizations, customers, technology, and more. Wiki pages also link to community spaces. Various topic domains in the MITREpedia site are fully searchable.

Bottom line: MITRE took a concerted approach to using 2.0 tools that connect all of its KM efforts into a seamless portfolio.

Royal Dutch/Shell

Royal Dutch/Shell's ask-learn-share behavioral model is the foundation for all of its KM and 2.0 activities. The approach emphasizes a cultural mind-set in which employees are encouraged to ask and search for information, as well as learn, improve, and share as they work.

The organization has three 2.0-driven KM components: METIS for relevant and quality assured information, the Shell Wiki for more details from many sources, and global networks for ad hoc knowledge sharing. The organization also has a number of supportive collaboration tools to increase networking opportunities while decreasing travel costs.

Blogging is in its early stages at Shell. Although blogging is not officially part of the KM portfolio, about 400 employees are currently blogging internally. Many of these researchers use blogs to document their research and experiments. And senior management uses blogs for internal communications.

Bottom line: Royal Dutch/Shell used 2.0 tools to drive the necessary behaviors for its KM program to excel in a global organization.

The U.S. Department of State

The State Department leverages a number of 2.0 tools for its employees.

Diplopedia, the State Department's enterprise wiki, offers a central place to share organizational knowledge with other intelligence agencies. The State Department also provides a knowledge-publishing platform driven at the grassroots level that integrates organizational knowledge. These community sites publish knowledge that otherwise would be confined to e-mail inboxes, document collections, and spreadsheets.

The State Department also has a messaging and archive retrieval toolset to support diplomacy through modern messaging, dynamic archiving, and information sharing. It combines a toolset for collaborating and searching and for integrating e-mails, cables, and memos. Employees can search archives and subscribe to alerts on selected topics, regions, or issues.

These efforts are bolstered by blog applications, search applications, and RSS feeds. The State Department also implemented IM,

Microsoft SharePoint, Documentum eRoom, Microsoft Groove, and InfoWorkSpace as collaboration tools for unclassified and classified environments.

Bottom line: The State Department leveraged 2.0 tools to change its entire organizational mind-set to a focus on knowledge sharing.

Closing Comments

An effective KM approach provides employees with exactly the information they need at exactly the moment they need it—their teachable moment. This should happen without undue disruption to the flow of work and critical knowledge. More and more, in the era of information overload, this involves distilling content into short, digestible chunks such as RSS alerts, wiki pages, discussion forum posts, and podcasts. With today's employees less willing to wade through databases and manuals, you must feed them information in a format that better serves their needs. This is where social computing will serve KM well.

The disdain and fear some still express for social computing is reminiscent of the objections we hear with the emergence of any new employee-empowering trend (e.g., teams in the 1970s, quality circles in the 1980s, and communities of practice in the 1990s). Then it goes mainstream and is incorporated into the way we work. This doesn't happen for all democratizing innovations, but we predict it will for social computing.

Let's now examine the ultimate user-driven element of Web 2.0: social networking.

Implementation Resources

The following APQC resources can help you implement these emerging approaches:

- Audio: *The Current Status of Enterprise 2.0 Adoption*
- *Centralized Search and Networking Portals*
- *Change Management Strategies for Enterprise 2.0 Tools*
- *Providing User-Driven Collaborative Tools*
- *Technology that Enables Knowledge Sharing*

(Continued)

- *The Role of Evolving Technologies: Accelerating Collaboration and Knowledge Transfer*
- *The Shifting Nature of Collaboration Tools*
- *Using Knowledge: Advances in Expertise Location and Social Networking*

These resources—along with APQC's custom advisory services and more than 1,000 articles focused on KM—are available at www.apqc.org and through this book's Web site at www.newedgeinknowledge.com.

Note

1. We think this is one of the best books written on the power and promise of social media for customer-facing applications: Josh Bernoff and Charlene Li, *Groundswell: Winning in a World Transformed by Social Technologies* (Boston: Harvard Business School Press, 2008).

CHAPTER

Working Social Networking

The rise of social networking has generated more commentary, analysis, and prophesying than any recent social phenomenon. Let's separate the hype from the facts.

> ## Social Networking
>
> *Social networking* refers to online places where users can create a profile and designate a network of people to see their posts and following their activities. Social networking is the pure manifestation of the user-driven philosophy.

The promise of user-driven computing is appealing to KM professionals. Cynics would say that *user driven* and *employee choice* are another way of saying, "Let's save some money and push the job off on employees." But we've found that employees enjoy the control as an adjunct to other approaches. Because communities of practice are the heart of KM, we believe social networks could become an important adjunct for creating and sustaining the engine of relationships and knowledge in a Web 2.0 world. Social networking also redefines *asset:* An asset can now be a relationship or a channel with the potential for other things to happen.

This chapter shares our perspectives and advice on how KM programs can best take advantage of social networking.

Guidelines for Enterprise Social Networking

Social Networking's Key Deliverable

Ruth McLenaghan, from IBM's Global Business Services, told APQC: "Social networking lets you use friends as filters. It gives users confidence in finding content and experts from people they trust."

Ride the Wave

Start or encourage employee groups on popular external sites like Facebook. Employees are connecting with colleagues on public sites. They are not going to stop. Leverage what is already happening organically so that you don't have to recreate it formally.

IBM Global Business Services currently has 4,000 Facebook groups and more than 22,000 employees on the IBM Facebook page. IBM finds that employees share more work-related discussions and have less personal interaction within the firewall. Providing access to both internal and external sites is beneficial, however, and IBM works to balance internal and external networks to maximize their value.

Baker Hughes Inc. established a private Facebook group that employees can join if they have a company e-mail address. High-potential employees join a Facebook group following training sessions so they can stay connected with colleagues across regions; this Facebook group is not controlled by the organization, and only training alumni are allowed to join.

Even organizations with strong security issues are forced to embrace social networking or be totally at its mercy. The U.S. Department of Defense, for example, recently authorized the use of Facebook and Twitter on nonsecure sites. The Department of Defense tracks all the Facebook pages created for its military services.[1] The U.S. Department of State is an active promoter of engagement with the public and its own staff through Facebook and Twitter.[2]

Your Organization Is Not Facebook

With our first piece of advice in mind, know that your employees don't need another Facebook. They already have that. Decide what they do need. Is it an easy way to create and use internal networks around topics or relationships? Is it an easy way to share information and documents with an ad hoc group? Or is it an easy way to continue networking after a face-to-face meeting? KM approaches start with the problems and opportunities identified in your knowledge strategy.

Don't expect frenzied participation. The rapid level of adoption and posting on social networking sites would be extremely challenging and very strange in a business context. Don't benchmark yourself against them. IBM's goal, for example, is to put the *work* back in social networking, so it doesn't expect 100 percent usage or exponential, viral growth.

Imitate What Works

Employees do want the same functionality they see on the most popular external Web sites. Adopt similar functionality internally, and replace or amend existing communities of practice and expertise location systems as appropriate.

It requires a paradigm shift to bring social networking inside the enterprise. Social networking tools allow informal groups to spring up. This may make managers uncomfortable, but it's a great way to generate new ideas and practices and empower employees.

IBM Global Business Services shifted its paradigm from formal communities to user-centered social networks. Its value proposition was to expedite and increase knowledge sharing, facilitate collaboration, and maximize the value of content. Utilitarian issues were also in play; this paradigm is less expensive than traditional content management. It reduces brokering and therefore costs.

Observe What Really Happens

In these early days of social networking, it is important to observe behavior and not let rosy theories cloud your vision about what employees will really do. Monitor and learn.

Not everything that works in a consumer space works in a business context. For example, your employees will probably not rate content in the way the general public does on Amazon. Your system is much smaller and less anonymous. (And giving your boss's PowerPoint presentation a lukewarm rating may not help your career.) You will need to observe behavior.

Collect data on usage, contacts, ratings, and so on from the beginning. This information helps elevate the most useful knowledge assets. Invest in and support what bubbles to the top in terms of value, and let the rest fall away. Relationships and posting behaviors can tell you a lot about what networks exist, which networks are vibrant (and therefore may deserve more support), and what content employees find valuable enough to share.

And don't try to prematurely define a return on investment, except for cost reduction from reduced content management. Wait until you understand the phenomenon in your own organization. Your colleagues may surprise you.

Trust but Verify

Some executives hear *social* and think frivolity. They fear employees will waste time, require special rules for control, and perhaps expose intellectual capital. Of course, the risk of employees wasting time or sharing proprietary information existed long before social networking. But the Internet does allow loose lips to sink many more ships (or as the saying now goes, loose tweets sink fleets).

You need some level of trust in employees' expected behavior, or you will spend more time policing their behavior than it is worth. However, consider just an occasional check to ensure that it hasn't become social *notworking*. For an enterprise social network, you can establish controls for behavior, content, and access, but it's unrealistic to expect a high level of control over the network itself. Come up with a simple governance mechanism and keep it light. Assume that existing records management best practices and e-discovery guidelines apply to all discourse conducted through social networks. You probably already have sufficient policies and guidelines for online business etiquette and for protecting intellectual property. Remind employees that they apply to social networking as well, both inside and outside the firewall. Communication and education are central to the solution.

Regarding privacy, adhere to the most restrictive privacy rules of any nation in which you have participating employees (e.g., often Germany or other European Union countries). Concerning international laws and requirements regarding the privacy of information, best-practice organizations researched by APQC found that the voluntary nature of the tools helps them comply. Employees can opt in or out of participating and sharing their information. They can also manage which information they choose to share about themselves.

Encourage Extended Networks

Who do you go to when you need information or expertise? Most employees will contact their immediate colleagues: members of their personal networks whom they already know and trust. KM professionals have long encouraged employees to leverage those networks while at the same time making new connections and building new relationships.

If employees broadcast a need or question only to their immediate network (often less than 150 people), then they may not be taking advantage of the best available input. When it comes to collaboration and networking, weak ties to more people are of greater benefit than strong ties to just a few people whom you know and may think like you do (Hansen 2009).

Because of its limitations, Fluor, ConocoPhillips, and Schlumberger avoided the friending element of social networking altogether by not leaving it to employees to select who is part of their large, global business communities. However, IBM Global Business Services does use the friending concept to allow IBM employees to establish their own networks and who can see their network. Using "Will you be my colleague?" requests to build one's network, IBM employees can see their network and friends of friends. Determine what best fits your KM strategy objectives.

Use Social Networking as an Adjunct to Expertise Location

We remember the early days of expertise location. The initial assumption was that employees would create profiles and designate themselves as experts. It didn't take long to find out that that wasn't going to work. Anything that relies on employees to fill out and maintain a form is going to be an exhausting struggle. And employees don't like the designation *expert;* it implies arrogance and invites scrutiny and extra work.

Expertise Location versus Social Networking

Expertise location is an integrated approach to identify people with expertise and link them to those with questions or problems, to assist workforce planning and project staffing, and to assist in career development. Social networking is an integrated approach to publicize skills, knowledge, interests, and activities; map existing relationships; and make this information available to others in order to create expanded networks.

In comes the promise of expertise location systems built on social networking and sophisticated tagging systems: to more easily connect employees, reduce the time needed to solve a problem, reduce ill-informed mistakes, help populate or update employees' profiles, and get employees up to speed faster. These new systems allow your employees to offer their experience when it suits them. They also balance formal and informal methods of expertise location, ranging from simple, directory-type applications to sophisticated algorithm-driven social networking approaches. The consistent features include:

- A centralized portal for numerous back-end services and data and knowledge repositories, supported by a federated search function
- An embrace of a portfolio of social computing tools (with the flexibility to adopt or dispense tools as needed)
- The use of automated processes and analytics that do not take employees out of their work flow

There are notable differences between expertise location and social networking, as outlined in Table 7.1.

Expertise location tools can still help your employees find *the* recognized experts in specific knowledge domains or disciplines or *the* authoritative content needed to answer questions. They appear to be more helpful when an employee knows what he or she is looking for. Social networking tools appear to be more helpful

Table 7.1   Comparing Expertise Location to Social Networking

Expertise Location	Social Networking
Formal, top-down designations	Informal, cross-boundary designations
Predefines the experts and expertise in a given domain (business-sponsored or selected experts)	Looks for experience across multiple domains (expertise inference)
Inflexible	Adaptive
Brokered	Self-service
Requires more resources to support	Requires fewer resources to support
Robust, stable enterprise suites	Open source, beta social computing tools
Centrally managed	User-driven and focused

when an employee needs to make a connection to answer some questions.

Closing Comments

If your business model requires access to deep domain knowledge, then it's probably worthwhile to continue to invest in a traditional KM approach. If your employees tend to be social media–savvy, then perhaps social networking is the engine that underpins KM for the foreseeable future. But social networking will probably not address your organization's full scope of KM needs.

There is no single, go-to strategy for implementing social networking across an enterprise. Government and private-sector organizations face different challenges with deployment and strategy. But the benefits of implementing social networking tools are just as real as the challenges. Social networks can connect employees in new and meaningful ways. It allows organizations to involve the customers and leverage existing product discussion groups and develop new communities of practice.

As social networking grows and evolves, we can expect to see multiple solutions surface to better connect employees. Social networks are just one tool in KM's continuing efforts to elevate an idea, threat, or opportunity to collective consciousness and a leadership priority—to connect the dots.

Implementation Resources

The following APQC resources can help you implement a social networking approach:

- *Don't Let Privacy Issues Stop Social Networking*
- *Measuring the Value of Social Networking Tools*
- *Social Networking in the Enterprise*
- *The Role of Evolving Technologies: Accelerating Collaboration and Knowledge Transfer*
- *Using Knowledge: Advances in Expertise Location and Social Networking*
- *Using Social Networking for Expertise Location: An APQC Overview*

These resources—along with APQC's custom advisory services and more than 1,000 articles focused on KM—are available at www.apqc.org and through this book's Web site at www.newedgeinknowledge.com.

Notes

1. U.S. Department of Defense social media site: www.defense.gov/RegisteredSites/SocialMediaSites.aspx.
2. U.S. Department of State social media sites: www.facebook.com/usdos and http://twitter.com/StateDept.

CHAPTER

Governance, Roles, and Funding

Y ou have laid out the enterprise strategy and approaches that will direct your organization's critical knowledge to where it needs to go. Now you need a supporting infrastructure. A KM program needs a governance model, roles to support the knowledge flow processes, and of course, funding. KM is all about people. But people cost money.

With our continuing focus on strategic concerns, this chapter addresses the key roles and how a KM program is typically funded, two areas usually of great interest to executives and KM professionals alike.

Governance Group

Your KM program needs a KM leader, a KM core group, design teams, and a governance group of sponsors and stakeholders (see Figure 8.1). The core group administers the KM program and KM approaches, whereas the governance group serves in a strategic and advisory capacity. Either executive level or cross functional, the governance group provides strategic oversight, direction, and resources.

Sometimes called an executive team, an advisory council, or a steering committee, the governance group's role for KM is to:

- Create purpose and context
- Guide strategy and the KM core group
- Approve large-scale funding and implementation of KM approaches

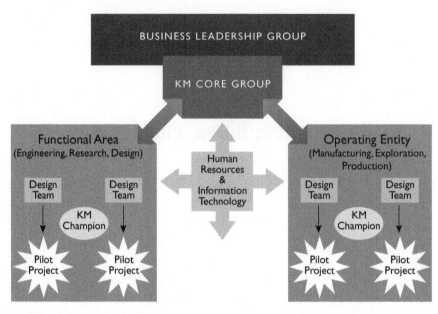

Figure 8.1   KM Program Governance Model

- Identify opportunities to support the overall organization
- Provide oversight on what is working and what is needed
- Attend to cross-cutting cultural issues and minimize barriers
- Model knowledge-sharing behaviors in high-profile roles
- Provide resources
- Encourage and celebrate role models and success stories

This governance group often includes business-unit leaders (or their lieutenants) and the chief information officer, as well as the KM leader and heads of organizational development, training, and HR functions. These people are not figureheads. Rather they are actively engaged in providing centralized support for standard processes and tools; importantly, they also ensure adoption of knowledge-sharing processes and principles.

The chief information officer, who focuses on physical computer and network assets, brings realistic expectations for what is hoped of your organization's existing infrastructure and what is possible to develop or buy.

The KM leader usually facilitates and guides the entire effort, acting as the link between the governance group and KM core group. But unlike most members of the KM core group with a specific functional interest, this position is focused on aligning behaviors and support structures with overall strategic goals.

The KM governance group is at its most active during the early days of developing the KM strategy and designing and implementing approaches. It ramps back up annually for strategic alignment, priorities, and resource allocation. The governance group guides the direction and scope of a KM program through sponsorship, funding, and monitoring in order to align the KM approaches with the organizational strategy. As design and development stabilize, the day-to-day role of your governance group drops into the background unless major issues arise.

ConocoPhillips and IBM have significant connections to executives and business leaders who are part of the overall governance structures. These top stakeholders are briefed by the KM core group and engaged in conducting regular knowledge-sharing events for their respective groups. They set top priorities but look to the KM core group to define, recommend, and guide as the (KM) process experts.

The primary accountability for enterprise KM typically lies with the KM core group.

KM Core Group

Sometimes called the core team or central support office, your KM core group makes KM approaches happen through tactical support and runs the day-to-day effort.

This group ideally acts as project managers for the implementation of your KM strategy and provides continuity along the way. At the business-unit level, the KM core group taps into localized needs and resources to understand social dynamics and to test new approaches. The KM core group also creates the training and education for other roles throughout the KM effort, as well as supports the appropriate tasks for sponsors, community leaders, and content managers.

The KM core group works in close partnership with IT, since no one to our knowledge has ever launched a global enterprise KM program without a robust IT platform. We found during APQC's study *The Role of Evolving Technologies* that best-practice organizations rely on their KM core groups to be the voice of employees and represent the knowledge-sharing needs of the workforce. IT functions then match those needs with the most appropriate applications.

The KM core group's responsibilities evolve as the KM program matures. They may involve:

- Securing executive endorsement and sponsorship
- Setting the budget and determining the resources necessary to support the KM infrastructure
- Fleshing out the KM business case and adhering to strategic direction based on organizational needs
- Designing and implementing roll-out plans
- Promoting common working standards and collaboration process standards using cross-functional input
- Defining common terminology and classification systems
- Creating common processes for knowledge documentation, categorization, and access
- Coordinating IT support and applications
- Enabling all KM approaches
- Recommending communication, training, rewards, and other issues affecting cultural acceptance of a KM approach
- Identifying and coordinating additional staff as needed, as well as specifying roles, measures, and training
- Providing methodologies including measurement support and reporting
- Creating a forum for surfacing, addressing, and solving shared KM issues and needs
- Defining technology to make knowledge reusable

Size of KM Core Group

You will need to find a level of KM staffing that is financially and culturally acceptable while also developing a network of resources from the business units.

We highly recommend that, in addition to the KM leader, this typically full-time core group include the following roles: a KM specialist, a KM communications director, and an IT/business analyst. Of course, some large enterprise KM programs have far more roles and full-time employees involved.

Let's look at these roles in greater detail. Providing clearly articulated roles and responsibilities ensures that your KM core group fully understands what actions they must take to be successful. Your KM program will falter without strong leadership and competency in these roles. (For each of the following roles, we provide more detailed job descriptions with competencies and skills at www.newedgeinknowledge.com.)

KM Leader

The KM leader oversees the KM program and the core group and ensures KM approaches align with and support your organization's strategic goals. This person is the face and social glue of your KM program, serving as the liaison among senior leaders and others involved in KM activities. Key responsibilities follow.

- Facilitates and supports KM strategy, business case development, vision, mission, and goals
- Facilitates and drives the development of your enterprise KM program
- Promotes KM and the use of common approaches across business units
- Works with business-unit leaders to establish a common understanding and focus for KM
- Provides KM thought leadership gained through projects, research, and benchmarking activities from internal and external opportunities
- Seeks out opportunities where knowledge sharing can add value to your organization

We've seen individuals excel in this role without previous expertise in KM. As long as the individual is a key contributor to your organization and willing to climb a steep learning curve if they are new to KM, the KM leader can rely on established KM best practices, methods, tools, and materials to develop expertise. (At APQC, we help such leaders all the time.)

KM Specialist

A KM specialist has skills and experience in the discipline of KM and its approaches. This person facilitates and coordinates the design and deployment of KM approaches, as well as the training and guidance of community leaders. The right-hand lieutenant to the KM leader, this person promotes KM as an organizational business practice and employee support system. Key responsibilities follow.

- Facilitates, monitors, and maintains the use and improvement of common KM approaches across your organization
- Monitors and reports progress of KM approaches to the KM leader
- Works with leaders to identify areas of opportunity and gaps in knowledge flow
- Supports the design, implementation, and enhancement of KM approaches
- Monitors and evaluates the KM program, including external benchmarking and evaluation programs and opportunities
- Monitors the effectiveness, maintenance, and use of the IT tools and systems as they apply to KM
- Disseminates information about the KM program to internal and external audiences

KM Communications Director

A KM communications director develops and manages communication to stakeholders regarding your KM program. This person works with other members of the KM core group and supporting roles to sustain awareness, seek out and publish success stories, and provide communications to and for leadership. Do not underestimate the value of this role. (You'll see why in Chapter 9.) Key responsibilities follow.

- Planning and leading communication strategy and efforts to strengthen awareness of knowledge-sharing benefits, behaviors, processes, procedures, successes, and tools
- Leading or participating in the planning of KM meetings, training, conferences, and special events
- Managing employee expectations for knowledge sharing through communication of KM approaches, progress, best practices, and opportunities for participation throughout your organization
- Sustaining the KM brand and themes with consistent, fit-for-purpose messaging

- Administering and supporting recognition programs when appropriate

IT/Business Analyst

An IT/business analyst supports your KM program as the liaison between the IT function and the KM core group, business units, and employees. Through collaboration with each of these stakeholders, the analyst ensures that the needs of your organization are met, employees receive the appropriate level of technology support, and corporate IT resources are effectively used. Key responsibilities of this essential role follow.

- Develops, implements, and supports the IT infrastructure in collaboration with the KM core group
- Supports the technology needs of KM-related leadership teams, business units, networks, and other stakeholders as needed
- Engages in and supports KM-related technology training and awareness activities
- Models best practices and knowledge-sharing behaviors in the use of enabling technologies

KM Design Teams

In addition to a KM core group, many best-practice organizations have approach-specific design teams. Sometimes the same as the KM core group, the design team takes into account organizational and cultural factors affecting the selected KM approach so it can better address knowledge needs and strategy issues. The design team should:

- Develop employee-related methods to gain participation
- Identify the critical content and how it will be managed
- Assess and leverage IT
- Develop approach-specific measures and a business case
- Finalize and manage the budget
- Launch and implement the KM approach

Design team members should be drawn from opinion leaders in your organization and operations areas who are engaged and passionate about using the KM approach to make their work outcomes better, more fun, and more satisfying. An enthusiastic, focused team is the one indispensable critical success factor for making a KM approach work. You will discover that a well-selected design team will provide a fresh perspective on knowledge flow.

When KM programs include a number of design teams, the KM core group usually will coordinate those teams and their customers and specialists so it can provide strategic oversight, direction, and resources. The KM core group can draw in various specialists from the business units to support the design teams.

Many other roles may need to be played as your KM program matures. At different times, you'll need various change agents, moderators, content managers, subject matter specialists, community leaders, consultants, facilitators, leaders, and even followers. Visit www.newedgeinknowledge.com for more descriptions and to adapt the responsibilities to fit your organization's structure and needs.

Investing in KM

Be prepared to invest in not only a KM core team and technology but also content management support, taxonomy development, employee communications and training, and other infrastructure demands. In addition to reallocating or hiring employees, your KM program will need funding to implement the approaches.

So what is this going to cost?

In APQC's studies *Successfully Implementing Knowledge Management* and *Measuring the Impact of Knowledge Management,* we asked best-practice organizations about their start-up and ongoing costs. The majority of global, multibillion-dollar organizations initially spent well over $1 million to implement their first KM program and spent the same amount annually to sustain it in the early years. Of course, your amount will be scaled to your organization depending on its objectives, scale, and scope and how integral the approaches are to your overall organizational strategies.

The best-practice organizations' median annual cost per KM participant was $152, but the median return per participant was $337. This return on investment (ROI) adds up quickly. Please keep in mind that the significant ROI found is not necessarily a function of maturity or length of time managing knowledge. The best-practice distinction is focusing KM approaches on organizational objectives and measuring the tangible outcomes.

Among the organizations with significant gains in their KM approaches, funding is higher from the inception of the KM program. Fluor's original KM budget and staffing was quite high. Now, the KM team currently operates on a much smaller budget than it did in 1999 when its enterprise KM program launched. This is possible because the team is able to leverage resources that did not exist 10 years ago. For example, community leaders, knowledge managers, and KM champions now exist across the organization to help the core team achieve its KM objectives.

In a late 2009 survey of APQC's KM practitioner community, 76 percent said the majority of their KM costs were for people. The remaining 24 percent said technology was their highest cost. However, only 8 percent said their total KM budget was part of their IT budget. The KM technology component was part of the IT budget for 34 percent of the respondents. A 57 percent majority said no part of their KM budget was part of the IT budget. Furthermore, even facing the worst recession in four decades, only 44 percent of KM budgets went down in 2009, and those declined an average of less than 10 percent.

There are numerous models for funding, both centralized and decentralized. Siemens' individual operating groups are responsible for funding their respective KM teams and dedicated KM improvement projects. At Shell, the individual businesses fund and resource KM implementation, and the central KM teams receive allocations to promote KM awareness and innovation. At the U.S. Department of State, KM is supported with a mix of base funding (provided to State's groups for basic operations of their KM approaches and activities) and central investment funds (to enable particular projects that may benefit the whole department). At Accenture, the KM core group is funded from the HR budget, but the IT element is funded from the CIO budget.

Balancing Corporate and Business-Unit Funding

APQC research shows that, when organizations launch a KM program and roll out the initial approaches, funding is often fully provided by a central or corporate group so it can remove money as a business-unit barrier to KM. However, over time, as the business units see value from KM and the time people spend, funding and support from business units increases and comes to balance out central funding.

Responsibility for the enterprise KM program office and KM core group and the technology infrastructure often continues to be funded by corporate. Time and labor may be charged back to the business units. Time and budgets for leading and participating in a KM approach is usually a business-unit investment, based on the experience that participation benefits the organization and helps employees.

At Schlumberger, Eureka communities are corporate-funded and cross-charged from the corporate budget. Community leaders are funded by the business units. The KM program office does not fund resources or time. Some events and community workshops receive funding from the program office, but such funding is minimal and expected to be matched by the business unit.

At Fluor, the KM team receives corporate funding for labor, expenses, Knowledge OnLine, and external software. This budget is allocated out to the businesses.

The ConocoPhillips central KM core group receives a budget for technology platforms; however, the business units pay for any costs associated with the employees who make up community teams (i.e., network leaders, sponsors, and core team members). Some networks receive initial funding to get started, but the expectation is that, eventually, funding will be distributed to the business units.

Making KM Valuable Enough to Fund

Dan Ranta from ConocoPhillips told APQC: "Our leaders understand the value of networks, and so they are willing to pay for them."

Closing Comments

It's easy for KM professionals to get caught up in the absorbing demands of developing an effective KM program infrastructure. But it's important to not lose sight of what this infrastructure enables. KM innovator (and this book's foreword contributor) Larry Prusak once shared with us some great funding advice: "If you have a dollar to spend on KM, go for connection instead of capture. It's a dollar better spent. [Having] more ways people can talk, more ways people can connect—and that means knowing who to talk to and connect with—is probably the best enabler."

In their zeal to get buy-in and get started, we've seen KM core groups underestimate the time and resources required for people, travel, and events. Ironically, they rarely seem to forget about the technology costs, probably because these are most tangible and an established budget exists for capturing them. Inadequate resources can mean slow development and less-than-stellar results and can signal to the general workforce that the senior leaders are not fully invested in the effort. For this reason, your KM core group needs to secure and fully leverage investments in infrastructure early on.

You need to create the most efficient—and effective—setup for your organization to connect employees and to put critical knowledge where they will trip over it. To be there at those crucial teachable moments, you'll need to facilitate the heck out of your KM program. A good infrastructure will help you do that. So will a sound change management effort, which we discuss in the following chapter.

Implementation Resources

The following APQC resources can help you implement a sound KM infrastructure:

- Audio: *Tough Economic Times and Your Knowledge Management Budget*
- *Defining Roles and Responsibilities for Community Leaders*
- *Governance Processes for Lessons Learned*
- *KM Core Team Job Descriptions*
- *Knowledge Management Program Key Teams*
- *Measuring the Impact of Knowledge Management*
- *Successfully Implementing Knowledge Management*
- *The Executive's Role in Knowledge Management*
- *The Role of Evolving Technologies: Accelerating Collaboration and Knowledge Transfer*
- *Using Structure/Roles to Drive Knowledge Management and Innovation*
- Video: *Adjust the KM Core Team as the KM Program Matures*

These resources—along with APQC's custom advisory services and more than 1,000 articles focused on KM—are available at www.apqc.org and through this book's Web site at www.newedgeinknowledge.com.

CHAPTER 9

Building a Knowledge-Sharing Culture

People, not technology, are the key to KM. Why?

First, sharing and learning are social activities. They take place among people.

Second, technology can capture descriptions but people can convey practices. Unlike simple descriptions, practices involve complex people, cultural, and contextual elements. Think of the differences between a map and the journey itself.

Third, to ensure practices and knowledge not only are shared but also are transferred effectively to make a difference, you have to connect employees who can and are willing to share the deep, rich, and tacit knowledge they have.

Across all cultures, mutual obligation and reciprocity are powerful social forces. Once employees start helping and sharing with one another, the effort becomes a self-perpetuating cycle.

We've seen a number of KM programs falter because KM professionals think they must first transform their organizational culture. Our response is to get over it. Culture change is more often a consequence of knowledge sharing than an antecedent to it.

In working with one of our government agency members, the senior leaders championing KM determined that it was about changing behaviors. They crafted detailed value statements calling for a change in behaviors and reported these out in a joint meeting with their direct reports and other key stakeholders. Although everyone agreed, nothing changed. The moral of the story is: Don't call for action if you can't back it up with your own actions. Be prepared to lead by doing, listening, and learning.

If your organization's natural tendency is to share and collaborate, then all you have to do is eliminate structural barriers and provide enablers (e.g., technology, facilitators, and standard approaches) to allow critical knowledge to flow where it needs to. But if your organization's tendency is to hoard knowledge, then the best and greatest KM approach may not be enough to alter your employees' behavior.

Your goal is to cultivate a knowledge-sharing culture while building capabilities for your KM program. That is, you focus on engaging, communicating with, and rewarding people, which builds the program and the culture.

There are three major ways to directly influence the norms and behaviors of employees as your KM program builds its capabilities: Lead by example; brand KM through thoughtful messaging, formal communications pushes, and rewards and recognition; and make KM fun. (Yes, we said fun!) This chapter examines these three efforts.

Knowledge-Hoarding Cultures

When knowledge is hoarded as power, you see limited interactions among employees, confined to a need-to-know basis. If employees do not trust coworkers or perceive that senior management is trying to capture knowledge so they can prepare for layoffs, then you will see virtually no knowledge transfer or contribution. If employees feel that knowledge should move only through the hierarchical structure or if groups perceive knowledge from other sources to be irrelevant, then you will see no breakdown in organizational barriers. If employees are only rewarded and promoted for the amount of knowledge they individually have, then they will not share. Address the barriers to sharing knowledge, not employees' attitude to the barriers.

Lead by Example

Executives are in a unique position to drive change. They are also in the best position to objectively determine whether knowledge is getting in the right hands and whether your organization is getting value from that.

We've observed that executive involvement lends credibility to KM programs and ensures the efforts will be long term. Leading by example, executives shape the values of your organization and establish a support system to initiate and manage change. Without direction from management, KM support tools and approaches are unlikely to align with your organizational strategy or be capitalized on for an intended purpose. Executives ensure that a KM program exists to support the big picture.

With such weight put on the shoulders of executives, it is encouraging to see that executives today have taken a more preemptive approach to KM and have not waited for grassroots efforts to proceed without an organization-wide vision. Enthusiasm like this is but one characteristic of leaders in organizations with the most successful KM programs.

We have found that organizations with successful KM programs have leaders from the CEO to mid-level management that regularly reinforce the need to share and leverage knowledge at every opportunity. We think that a desire to learn, on the part of executives, is important not only as an example to employees but also as a sign that the leaders are dedicated to cultivating a knowledge-sharing culture. We have found that senior managers truly committed to learning most likely have already laid the groundwork for a knowledge-sharing culture. These same leaders are also more likely to allocate adequate resources to support KM.

For example, when Schlumberger senior leaders visit field service operations, they want to see not only where best practices have been identified but also where employees in the field have adopted best practices found in Schlumberger's InTouch system. Consequently, all field service employees feel compelled to engage with other employees and look for opportunities to improve.

At Fluor, leaders—and how they communicate—play an important role in sustaining a knowledge-sharing culture. Fluor's executive leaders consistently communicate the value and importance of sharing knowledge, which has a profound impact on KM efforts. Fluor's CEO and executives frequently promote tools such as its online portal and communicate the importance of knowledge sharing in speeches and reports.

Determine what types of leaders your KM champions are, and then use those strengths to support your KM program. Our KM Advanced Working Group identified 10 desirable types of leaders for KM.

1. *Progressive leader.* Responds to and supports new ways of creating, capturing, and sharing information (e.g., approves budgets, charge codes, and resources; investigates new methods; communicates value of approaches; and ensures employees have the knowledge, skills, and resources they need).
2. *Investigative leader.* Seeks out and listens to divergent perspectives at multiple levels both inside and outside the organization.
3. *All-for-one leader.* Breaks down organizational silos (e.g., cross-functional working and shared objectives and budgets).
4. *Trusted leader.* Promotes trust through consistency, follow-through, and fairness (e.g., through messaging, application of rules and policies, and keeping commitments).
5. *Methodical leader.* Uses and encourages others to use collaborative tools, methods, and KM approaches.
6. *Visionary leader.* Communicates goals of the organization, function, or project in a way that others can align with.
7. *Implementation leader.* Translates strategy to enable teams to develop and implement knowledge-sharing tactics.
8. *Observant leader.* Recognizes and rewards outcomes and collaborative behavior (e.g., catch in-the-act good behavior, share success stories, and match a reward to the personality of an employee).
9. *Innovative leader.* Uses approaches to tap the creativity of others (e.g., mind mapping, brainstorming, and the nominal group technique).
10. *Follower-centric leader.* Inspires self confidence in followers, clearly communicates direction and performance expectations, involves followers in the planning process, demonstrates respect and concern for others, and values unique qualities of employees as an asset for working together.

Both the KM core group and senior leaders should be aware of your organization's current cultural state (and the extent of the need to change behaviors). Identify what dynamics will support change, as well as what barriers can be expected. A yellow flag should be raised if you cannot answer the following questions with confidence.

- Are employees receptive to learning opportunities?
- Does your organization make a point to hire intellectually curious employees?
- Do employees feel their job is no less secure by sharing information and revealing mistakes made?
- Are settings to identify mistakes and lessons learned separate from individual evaluations?
- Are problems and opportunities addressed in a collaborative manner?
- Do employees feel as if no business topic is too sensitive to discuss?
- Do employees feel that they can approach any level of manager within your organization?
- Is the opportunity to explore new and innovative ideas a part of each employee's workday?
- Do employees identify as much with your organization as with their individual professions?
- Are employees given time to teach each other? Is teaching and mentoring a factor in promotions?
- Do the major work flows through your organization enable employees to frequently interact?
- Do managers encourage and respect different opinions and suggestions for improvements?
- Do business units recognize that relevant information may come from other units and external sources?
- Do managers encourage their employees to help employees in other units?
- Does senior management understand the reason for differences in values among units and subgroups?
- Do employees understand the long-term benefits to sharing what they know?
- Are employees who provide innovative ideas recognized or rewarded?
- Are employees who collaborate and build off others' ideas recognized or rewarded?
- Are team-based performance and accomplishments recognized along with individual accomplishments?

An answer of "no" to any of these questions may be the unintentional result of specific policies and management approaches throughout your organization. For instance, why would a workforce not be receptive to learning opportunities? Is it because they have pressure to perform on specific goals, without any managerial expectations for professional development? Is individual expertise more valued than assisting or mentoring others? Has your organization failed to provide training opportunities or encourage employees to expand their responsibilities?

The KM core group must be able to answer these questions to gauge resistance and take appropriate steps for implementation of the KM program. Senior leaders must be able to answer these questions to carry out in an informed manner their crucial responsibilities for communications.

The KM core group may be able to recognize certain barriers, but it will likely be within the executive domain to aggressively eliminate counterproductive policies. This may involve tracking training on balanced scorecards, rewarding collaborative efforts over the lone hero, directing your organizational development function to expand employees' learning opportunities and managers' expectations, spelling out for the human resources function what qualities you want in new employees, and making an example at the top by tying promotions to knowledge-sharing behaviors.

Brand Aggressively

To develop a knowledge-sharing culture, you need consistent messaging, a formal and pervasive communications push, and reinforcement of desired behaviors through rewards and recognition. At every milestone of KM deployment, employees need examples of success so they can justify dedicating their time to leveraging new technology and changing specific behaviors. What you need, we're telling you, is a *brand* to rally the troops and to lessen confusion about how KM fits into your organization.

Don't Let Your Software Brand Your Program

We have seen many KM programs get branded by their technology application and then crash and burn. A wiki is a tool, not a brand to promote your KM program. Ensure that KM is seen as a holistic approach enabled by dedicated employees, standard processes, and robust technology tools.

Language Matters

You'll need to develop messaging that resonates with your organization's culture. This is different from many approaches to change management during the past two decades, when the look and feel of the change program itself was laid on top of the organizational culture. Instead, you should radically adapt the look and feel of your KM brand to the style of your organization.

Some organizations talk directly about the importance of sharing knowledge; have official knowledge-sharing events, sponsors, and structures; sanction communities of practice; and conduct internal advertising. Others avoid using any term like *knowledge management* that could imply a vendor solution or could invoke a not-invented-here reaction. And some KM champions actively avoid the term *knowledge* and frame their program only in internally accepted business terms. (For example, "We're going to reduce cycle time by finding new ways to reuse our engineering designs.") Or they may simply focus on the most tangible KM elements first. Many best-practice organizations have a branded name for their KM efforts, such as *collaboration* and *knowledge networks*. Any of these approaches can bring the workforce on board if the cultural elements fit.

Organizations rarely have a monolithic culture: Various micro-cultures thrive. And these cultures can vary widely. The culture in the sales organization will not be the same as research and development, which is why we recommend that design team members for KM approaches be a representative sample of the cultures KM will find itself. Values influence employees' perceptions of knowledge and the extent to which it should be managed. Different perceptions of the importance of KM principles can lead to conflict, and divergent subgroups need to be taken into consideration. Determine where it's possible to standardize messaging, but remain open to adapting your language to reach specific microcultures as well.

Consider the example provided by Ernst & Young. Each employee, when hired, is given an agreement outlining his or her responsibilities regarding sharing insights with colleagues. Knowledge-sharing policies also explain the behavior expected of employees and provide guidance on managing client confidentiality while adhering to information-sharing requirements. The fact that knowledge-sharing competencies are integrated into employees' annual goals serves as a reminder that the organization takes KM seriously.

Communication

Branding requires a communications plan. Don't take this for granted. You want KM to be viewed as a mode of operations, not another initiative that requires additional time or resources. This is why you have a KM communications director.

Your workforce will need frequent communications to understand and participate in your KM approaches. Communications concerning what your KM program stands for and what behaviors are desired should precede any specific messaging of your organization's output goals. Your communications plan should leverage messages for all audiences: from the highest to the lowest levels of your organization; from the most to least formal interactions; and from the least to the most diverse groups. You can integrate messages into existing outlets such as newsletters, Web pages, and events. Figure 9.1 provides a template to align all such messages in a strategic communications plan.

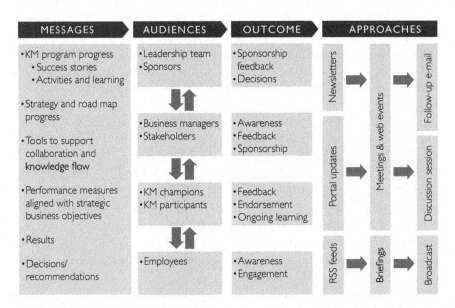

Figure 9.1   Communications Plan Template

To ensure your communication plan is effective:

- Use multiple channels to disseminate messages: Cascade the communication plans throughout your organization using Web pages, publications, management meetings, presentations, and so on.
- Develop an elevator speech for KM champions and managers (a five-point, two-minute overview of how KM can improve results).
- Use stories and external benchmarks to create compelling images for the benefits of collaboration.
- Make a communication plan part of each function's tactical plans for collaboration. (To do this, identify stakeholders that must be communicated with and include daily, weekly, and monthly communication ideas, as well as key leadership messages.)
- Use training to disseminate collaborative principles. Training is integral to successful change management and will reinforce key messages.

Knowledge-sharing events are a way to energize and fully brand your KM efforts. It doesn't necessarily link to an employee's or group's performance but could have a big impact on connecting people to one another, which in turn enables collaboration.

At ConocoPhillips, communicating the value and purpose of its KM approaches is recognized as critical to engaging employees. The organization's designated communications adviser coordinates all KM communication efforts. For example, the adviser uses the organization's central portal to share news and discussions, as well as showcase award recipients and community of practice leaders.

Like other organizations with high turnover and role changes, Ernst & Young faces challenges in keeping the value of knowledge sharing top-of-mind for its employees. To address this, it created formal knowledge-sharing expectations through agreements and policies and engaged line leaders to help shape and reinforce individual knowledge expectations, with everyone ultimately sharing the responsibility of being a knowledge worker.

Reward and Recognize

You will also need to reward and recognize knowledge-sharing behaviors. Rewards and recognition address the universal question,

"What's in it for me?" They also help communicate what is really important to your organization. Employees should be rewarded for sharing what they know, and functions should be rewarded for fostering collaboration.

So that we're clear on this issue: Best-practice organizations do not see rewards and recognition as a Pavlovian method to motivate employees to share. Instead, they see it as a way to acknowledge the value of sharing knowledge, appreciate the contributions employees have made, and increase awareness of the importance of sharing knowledge.

At Fluor, community membership engagement is celebrated through peer recognition programs. Its KM Pacesetter program recognizes community members who actively submit knowledge, act as members, and suggest improvements to the knowledge community. Employees are nominated by their peers and receive a plaque and recognition for community participation. This program reinforces community engagement.

Another key component is Fluor's annual "Knowvember" knowledge campaign. During the month of November, community members submit global success stories, nominate members for outstanding community involvement, and participate in KM workshops around the world.

Some general principles for rewarding and recognizing knowledge-sharing behaviors follow.

- Create recognition for collaborating, sharing, transferring, and using knowledge and best practices. You can do that by celebrating best-practice success stories and propagating tales of big savings and important contributions.
- The time needed to collaborate with others has to be recognized and rewarded. If participants feel that they have to steal time from "real" work, then collaboration will not occur.
- Employees have to get value out of collaborating, be it knowledge they need or a sense of status and recognition.
- Recognize everyone involved, including those who share knowledge and those who receive knowledge. If both ends are not feeling rewarded, then desired results will not be accomplished.
- A standardized reward system may help institutionalize new behaviors into the common culture.

The appropriate approach to rewards and recognition varies across the levels of KM program maturity. In the early levels, resources and recognition can be less formal. However, as your KM capabilities mature, you can tie rewards to formal KM measures and knowledge-sharing behaviors to employee performance appraisals. Such apprais-als are possible once your KM program has successfully embedded knowledge-sharing behaviors into employees' work flow.

For example, one of 3M's criteria for promotion in the research and development arena is knowledge sharing, demonstrated by par-ticipation and leadership in its communities of practice, writing and publication, speeches, and mentoring. 3M's Tech Center employees are expected to capture lessons and increase 3M's knowledge base for future innovation. And employees are evaluated by how many divisions they persuade to adapt a technology platform into products (knowledge transfer from the laboratory to the business).

ConocoPhillips's KM program linked knowledge sharing to busi-ness results based on "the four Gs": *give* (share your knowledge with others), *gather* (collect knowledge from colleagues and available resources), *grab* (be willing to ask questions and look externally for knowledge), and *guts* (lessons learned). As a result, its number of KM success stories grew exponentially.

Your assessment and understanding of your culture and how it responds to formal versus informal rewards and recognition will help you address this issue.

Make KM Fun

If KM is so critical to success, why do you also need to make it fun?

Because fun can make your KM efforts thrive. We're not talking about handing out silly hats or wearing Hawaiian shirts on Friday. We're talking about injecting creativity, experimentation, play, and innovation into everyday knowledge transfer and the promotion of KM approaches.

Fun is one of the key components of life, but it is easily lost in business. Employees face a lot of pressure and demands for their time. Simply reawakening your employees' sense of humor can moti-vate them to share their knowledge.

When you inject fun into the work flow, you begin to boost creativity and innovation by creating space—or breathing room—in the normal cadence of operations. Laughing together builds cooperation. It breaks employees out of their normal modalities and boosts morale. A good laugh even changes our body chemistry. And all of that increases our productivity when we allow fun to be part of our work experience.

This is why it is important to make KM tools and approaches fun to learn about and fun to use.

How do we make KM fun?

- *Make KM tools and approaches engaging.* Determine what it takes to keep your target audience engaged. Are your KM tools a chore to use? Or are they engaging, relevant, and novel?
- *Use humor.* Humor promotes creativity and innovation. Establishing a playful tone can make your audience more comfortable contributing their knowledge. It's also a great tool to address skepticism and ultimately bolster KM adoption. The bottom line is that humor is one of the most effective ways to grab someone's attention.
- *Introduce friendly competition.* Turn a task into a game. Challenge your audience to use your KM tools and participate in KM approaches by playfully testing the skills and competencies they excel at in day-to-day work. KM messaging that includes the element of playful competition among peers allows an audience to have fun sharing knowledge while showing off their own capabilities.
- *Seek inspiration elsewhere.* Look outside the business world to find fun. For example, take something like a popular song or commercial out of context and apply it to your organizational environment. By leveraging your audience's external interests, you can increase your message's relevance and secure more attention for your KM tools and approaches.
- *Enable two-way interaction.* When you set an example of creativity, experimentation, play, and innovation, your audience is emboldened to embrace those values. Encourage your audience to experiment with KM tools and ways to share knowledge, actively solicit their input, and publicize how you are using that feedback to make your KM tools and approaches fun to learn about and use.

The following examples show how serious organizations make KM not only relevant but also fun for their employees.

IBM has secured high adoption rates for KM through fun campaigns that garner attention. For example, IBM created a video to convey the top 10 reasons to use its practitioner portal. It's a quick, humorous video designed to drive adoption. The campaign worked because it had substantial general appeal. It was concrete, work related, useful, funny, and short.

Another example is IBM's Einstein challenge. In 2009, IBM began transitioning to a new interface for its knowledge repository. To motivate employees to use the new interface, IBM created another quick, humorous video to drive contributions and bring employees to the portal. Using a link and an e-mail push, the campaign quickly garnered views. The e-mail's subject line asked: "Are you smarter than Einstein?" The e-mail encouraged employees to log on to the portal and take the Einstein challenge. And the embedded minute-and-a-half video encouraged employees to contribute the best knowledge assets on their hard drives. It drove behavior that led to spikes in usage and a lasting upswing in usage.

These examples show relatively inexpensive ways to make KM fun to learn about. Having studio-quality videos is not as important as making the message brief, humorous, and relevant.

The second organizational example of making KM fun comes from the Federal Reserve Bank of Cleveland. Fun and banking may seem like an oxymoron. This organization has proved that thinking wrong.

The Federal Reserve Bank of Cleveland's KM core team planned a highly publicized event to promote its KM tools and the appropriate use of those tools. The hour-long event was formatted in the style of a popular TV game show. Drawing in participants with lunch and small prizes, the team took a simple, low-cost approach by staging the game show using staff as contestants. The audience learned about collaboration tools in a fun setting.

The Federal Reserve Bank of Cleveland also planned a virtual scavenger hunt that helped participants become familiar with its KM tools. Participants received a card with types of knowledge to look for online. The challenge played to the audience's strengths.

By applying well-known cultural references—TV shows—in a new context and encouraging competition, the efforts ultimately bolstered usage of the organization's KM tools. This momentum is maintained through similar quarterly events such as a networking event humorously styled like speed dating.

Such efforts make KM tools fun to use and, ultimately, make for more productive employees.

Closing Comments

KM is serious business. The ability to secure enduring value from intellectual assets determines winners and losers in the marketplace. And the winners usually have a knowledge-sharing culture.

A knowledge-sharing culture just feels better and it works better. In a knowledge-sharing collaborative culture, employees freely create, share, and use information and knowledge; they work together toward a common purpose; and they are supported and rewarded for doing so. Employees who collaborate and share knowledge are also better able to achieve their work objectives, do their jobs more quickly and thoroughly, and receive recognition from their peers and mentors as key contributors and experts.

Let's now examine how to gauge such impact.

Implementation Resources

The following APQC resources can help you foster a knowledge-sharing culture:

- *Developing a Knowledge-Driven Organizational Culture*
- *Encouraging Participation in Your Organization's Lessons Learned Approach*
- "Our Edge in Knowledge Sharing," Presented by ConocoPhillips's Dan Ranta at APQC's 2008 KM Conference
- *Rewarding and Recognizing Collaboration*
- *The Dirty Dozen: Worst Collaborative Behaviors Quiz*
- *Using Knowledge Management to Drive Innovation*
- Video: *Communications Breed Cultural Change*

These resources—along with APQC's custom advisory services and more than 1,000 articles focused on KM—are available at www.apqc.org and through this book's Web site at www.newedgeinknowledge.com.

CHAPTER

10

Measuring the Impact of Knowledge Management

A reporter called us recently to ask about our work in measurement. She said she regularly hears that organizations don't know how to measure KM. We find this frustrating given the amount of time APQC spends helping KM professionals do just that. APQC has benchmarked KM measures for more than 15 years and found numerous successful measurement systems. Those organizations that most rigorously measure KM can show a 200 percent return on investment (ROI)—a healthy return by any standard.

Yet measurement continues to intimidate many. Challenges arise from measurement practices being decentralized and ad hoc. We also often hear that it is difficult to isolate the impact of KM, link measures to investments, standardize KM measures for comparison, and secure data (much less the resources needed to secure that data) from those using KM tools. Measurement isn't always easy, but few things worthwhile are.

Measures are not just for looking good; they should help you make decisions, take corrective action, adjust your course, or improve your processes. And yes, they should ultimately show an impact on overall strategic goals. A finely honed KM measurement system will help to:

- Align KM with your organizational strategy
- Determine progress
- Prioritize KM investments
- Evaluate and communicate about performance

- Tie participation and learning to outcomes
- Demonstrate the capabilities of KM approaches
- Educate employees about critical knowledge flow and how to improve it
- Establish the accountability required for critical knowledge to flow where it's needed
- Gauge behavioral changes and acceptance of KM as a business practice

This chapter details types of measures, how to select the right measures, how to analyze results, the importance of systematically approaching KM measurement, and what to expect over the long haul.

Don't Skip This Chapter!

As KM enters the mainstream of management practices, KM investments must satisfy the same business case requirements as every other investment. When APQC started studying KM in its early stages, a program might get launched and funded on vision and promise, but in a climate of ever-increasing emphasis on productivity and effectiveness, KM is not exempt from scrutiny. It is so important for your KM program to not only deliver value but also demonstrate that value in concrete terms. You need to know which approaches produce a return and which do not, as well as where to focus efforts and where to invest. As your KM program matures, so will your measurement practices and your ability to demonstrate a tangible impact on overall strategic goals.

A Portfolio of Measures

Make this your mantra: Your organization's strategic goals drive your KM program. This is not a loose connection; it's a direct link. Your portfolio of measures confirms that link.

Most KM measurement attempts fall short of tying KM program efforts to business outcomes. The gap results from not using a framework to develop measures in the initial phases of KM program development and not being clear about the specific business objectives to be achieved. This relative fuzziness leads to KM approaches that are not as crisply designed or deployed as they could be. During APQC's study *Measuring the Impact of KM,* we found that best-practice organizations, on the other hand, directly tie KM program efforts to measures clearly associated with cost savings or revenue generation.

Each KM approach requires its own set of measures. The measures used for KM approaches are often the measures that get rolled up or aggregated and reported as a subset of the KM program measures.

Your portfolio of KM measures can be divided into three basic categories.

1. *Activity measures.* These are measures of involvement. KM approaches embedded in the work flow provide a legitimate reason to measure use and participation. Communities of practice would require different measures (e.g., response time to questions posed among community members) from measures for a content management system (e.g., the number of downloads or submissions).

2. *Process efficiency measures.* These measures ensure critical knowledge is flowing where it needs to for it to drive strategic goals. These measures help you monitor and understand how your KM approaches help the knowledge flow so that you can make course corrections. For example, a KM program with a lessons-learned approach might track the duration of and effort involved in the capture process, participant satisfaction, and the reuse of lessons.

3. *Business performance measures and outputs.* These measures evaluate the performance of your business operations and activities. They will provide the link from KM program efforts to organizational results. For example, a KM program with collaboration approaches to improve a sales process might align with revenue growth and track sales-win rates, information available for a needs analysis per sales proposal, and number of contributions (tips and best practices) to a sales wiki.

Try to identify measures across all three categories to ensure a complete set of information that is aligned, is actionable, and tells a complete story. But don't measure everything that moves. Focus on relevant data with direct links to overall strategic concerns. But don't wait for the perfect measures in order to begin. Fail fast and correct course, and the data will get cleaner over time.

When it comes to KM measures, don't recreate the wheel. APQC does have standard measures for common KM approaches as a starting point (www.newedgeinknowledge.com). However, the business performance, output, and outcome measures will differ by organization. The most effective KM measurement systems begin with an organization's strategic goals and measures and then work backward to create measures for KM approaches. *Your* KM strategy will drive you to the right measures for each approach.

For example, IBM's KM core group follows these eight steps:

1. Determine organizational objectives and strategy and how the KM approach will help achieve those goals.
2. Determine the purpose of the KM approaches to be implemented.
3. Determine how the measures will be used and who will use them.
4. Determine which measurement framework (balancing leading and lagging indicators or quantitative and qualitative data) is best.
5. Determine what should be measured.
6. Determine how the measures will be collected and analyzed.
7. Determine what can be learned from the measures and what actions should be taken.
8. Revisit the organizational objectives and align measurements.

At a high level, you want measures that will ensure you are meeting the following criteria for a mature measurement system:

- KM aligns with the organization's vision, mission, and strategy.
- KM is recognized as a competitive differentiator.
- KM is accounted for in your organization's budget.
- KM resources are embedded throughout your organization.
- KM governance is conducted at senior leader levels.
- KM is an integral element of your organization's learning and improvement strategies.
- KM value is recognized as a brand.
- KM is embedded both above and in the flow of work.
- KM is considered a core competency of your organization.

- KM capabilities ensure that expertise is available and accessible.
- KM IT tools ensure organization-wide access while protecting your organization's intellectual capital.

Now, let's look at measures in the context of APQC's levels of knowledge management maturity to determine your organization's capability and maturity to measure KM going forward.

Do You Have a KM Measurement Problem?

- Are your KM tools and activities dispersed and decentralized?
- Are your KM measures ad hoc or localized?
- Do you lack standard KM measures to use for comparison?
- Do you struggle with attributing the impact of KM approaches on outcomes?
- Do you lack data from business or functional units that use KM approaches?
- Is your link between organizational results and KM investments weak?
- Do you lack the appropriate resources to help you capture KM and business output data?

Visit www.newedgeinknowledge.com to see how APQC can help.

Measuring across the Levels of Maturity

It is never too soon to track how KM creates value for your organization.

Measures will vary, however, across the levels of KM program maturity. (See Chapter 3 for a general description of each level.) In its early days, any KM program needs measures of acceptance, behavioral changes, and alignment with business strategy. As your KM program matures, you will need more sophisticated tools and processes for analysis as well as methods to predict and track desired outcomes. What you start out with will not be what you end up with.

It's time to get started.

Level 1: Initiate—Growing Awareness

With no KM approaches or supporting KM activities yet in place, you will have few or no KM measures at this level. But you should have a vision of how the flow of critical knowledge can add value to your organization.

When you are just getting started, compelling examples of success are memorable and start to demonstrate how KM can help your organization. Stories can help communicate the need to change and improve. They can also establish the causal link among inputs, behaviors, and outcomes for the business case and measurement reporting process.

The ability to tell meaningful stories will continue to be important as you expand and improve your measurement capabilities. However, stories will not be sufficient to establish a solid business case for continued investment in KM beyond Level 3.

Level 2: Develop—Growing Involvement

As you begin implementing your KM strategy and designing or leveraging KM approaches that help knowledge assets flow, you will be able to measure participation. KM measurement at Level 2 should focus on participation metrics such as the number of contributions to a best practices repository, the number of documents downloaded, and the number of employees who participate in a community of practice. It's common for measures to include yes or no questions about completion of activities, such as having a charter for each of your communities or completion of a milestone defined in your KM strategy. There are also the less tangible, but measurable benefits from reuse of materials and expertise, eliminating redundant efforts, avoiding repeated mistakes, and finding information quickly and easily. These early measures can validate the business case and determine what is and isn't working.

For example, Schlumberger routinely collects and reviews activity measures for its Eureka communities. Typical data include membership growth, the number of profiles accessed, links to knowledge, frequency of updates, and the number of supplier visits and field trips.

Although activity measures are critical indicators of the usefulness of KM approaches, they are not an end in themselves. They must be linked with activities and outputs of business processes and performance.

Level 3: Standardize—Aligning Processes and Approaches

By Level 3, your KM program has identified the value path for how KM approaches affect overall strategic goals. APQC's Input-Outcome

Measurement Model (see Figure 10.1) aligns and traces the value path of KM to organizational results. The framework provides a map to trace KM investments (inputs), participation (process and behaviors) to outputs, and bottom-line measures (outcomes). An inability to trace the value of a KM approach is a red flag to reexamine the intent and implementation of the approach.

APQC's Measurement Alignment Worksheet can help determine those inputs, processes, outputs, and outcomes (see Figure 10.2). The tool allows you to show (and think about) the relationships along the value path. Depending on the desired KM behavior, examples of inputs might include time, salaries, and IT costs. KM activities and approaches may be measured through participation, contribution to a body of knowledge, and applied practices. Process outputs align with critical factors for success such as improved cycle time to market and faster invoice payment. Examples of outcomes important to your organization might include employee and customer retention, reduced costs per transaction, and increased revenue. With this information in hand, you can illustrate how KM behaviors drive outcomes.

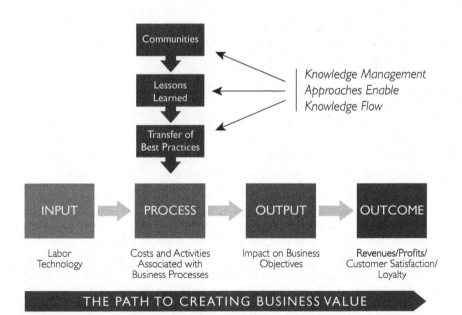

Figure 10.1   APQC'S Input-Outcome Measurement Model

Organizational Goals	Business Outputs	Major Business Processes & Performance Measures	KM Approaches & Performance Measures
		Process	KM Approach
		M1	M1
		M2	M2
		Process	KM Approach
		M1	M1
		M2	M2
		Process	KM Approach
		M1	M1
		M2	M2
		Process	KM Approach
		M1	M1
		M2	M2

Figure 10.2   APQC's Measurement Alignment Worksheet

Our best advice at this level is to keep the measures reasonable in scope and number. In addition to keeping it simple, it is also important to measure strategically. In other words, don't spend too much time collecting data and not enough time understanding what it means or what actions it should drive.

Level 4: Optimize—Driving Organizational Outcomes

Measures at Level 4 should focus on the return on investment and using performance predictors. To establish a financial link between KM efforts and overall strategic objectives, consistently conduct quantitative analyses of knowledge flow processes, KM approaches, and their impact on business performance and business outputs.

The dollar value of other results—such as cost avoidance, customer satisfaction, cycle-time reduction, quick problem resolution, and professional development and morale—can also be calculated, but the effort is greater. We recommend that you select the most tangible calculations to capture gains. These alone are often sufficient to justify the cost of your KM program.

We suggest integrating such KM measures into your organization's performance scorecard. This ensures your KM program focuses on strategic objectives and measures tangible outcomes.

Level 5: Innovate—Continuously Improving Practices

At Level 5, clear business outcomes justify continued investment in the KM program. Your measures should enable you to take predictive and innovative actions. The requirement for taking these actions is making meaning of the data.

Consider how Fluor measures its KM approaches. In line with its overall strategic goals, Fluor tracks revenue per employee as a measure of productivity. Furthermore, enhanced revenue streams are correlated with the extensive connectivity their KM efforts have created. A single success story from Fluor illustrates how the expertise found in a community not only resulted in savings of €1 million for a project but also led to additional work of nearly the same magnitude due to the client's confidence in Fluor's knowledge.

At ConocoPhillips, the documented, tangible effect of communities on the bottom line (through cost savings and other benefits) has totaled in the hundreds of millions of dollars—not a surprising achievement given that more than 5,000 success stories have been documented and verified.

And as far back as 2003, Schlumberger was reporting savings to the organization of approximately $150 million per year due to expertise sharing through its technical communities of practice. Schlumberger's knowledge-sharing and collaboration efforts have led to a 95 percent average reduction in the time required to solve technical problems.

The Power of Analytics

The holy grail of KM measurement is to tie participation to outcomes. We sometimes run experiments for APQC clients between two otherwise similar groups or regions in order to determine whether their results differ based on how much KM participation is under way. (It does.) We've also found it useful to examine results from one group over time to see how well the correlations with business outcomes hold up, even when causality is not something we can prove. From such analytics, you can determine if your KM program truly makes a difference. The more employees participate in KM activities, share and use information, and adopt practices, the more you can correlate KM activities with organizational outcomes. Time and again, we have seen just that.

So can you make the leap directly from participation to organizational outcomes? No. But given the tools we discuss in this chapter, you can trace the value path (of what behavior is supposed to be correlated with what output) and then define it with key measures and indicators of performance. Then, you use statistical analysis such as cross-tabulation, correlation plots, and regression analysis to demonstrate the relationships between KM efforts and process performance, as well as relationships between process performance and organizational outcomes.

(Multiple factors may influence process-level performance and organizational outcomes and, thus, your interpretation of the statistical results. You will need to engage your stakeholders to provide input for clarity on the potential impacts of these factors on findings from the data.)

These insights will support your business case for your KM program and approaches. This becomes the basis to formulate your data-driven recommendations to improve KM and organizational performance.

A key to ensure effective buy-in for your KM measurement activities is to produce a concise and usable report-out of findings on a regular basis. We recommend that reporting include synthesized analysis of concise findings that are relevant to a specific audience, depicted through graphs, tables, and narration. Ensure graphical integrity, be clear, and tell a motivational story.

A KM Measurement System

No matter what level you are at, lists of measures alone won't do you any good. You will need processes and accountability for collecting, organizing, reporting, and acting on the measures to improve your KM program, as well as to provide the basis for funding and investment. Such a measurement system should ultimately capture intangible measures—such as social cohesion, job satisfaction, and time to competency—that will provide a broader perspective of successful KM efforts. A measurement system provides a framework to present a common understanding of the current situation, what needs to be done to improve, and how progress is going to be measured and rewarded.

You will need to tap in to your current organizational measurement systems or begin developing one that will support your ongoing KM measurement. Your KM measurement system will work best if you embed it into the flow of daily operations.

Your KM measurement system should feed your target audience the information required. Success in measuring KM is about 20 percent process and 80 percent change management. The measurement system has to involve people. Helping employees understand the analytics and potential results will promote dialogue and uncap the potential of those results. Dedicated employees, resources, and processes for key measurement activities—such as collecting, analyzing, and reporting—will be needed, but assign responsibility for action and resources to process owners as well.

Remember that measures provide different value to different stakeholders. Senior executives and financial leaders are interested in the link to desired outcomes, KM program leaders are interested in rates of participation, and participants are interested in operating measures that affect their ability to do their jobs. Work with your stakeholders and process owners to engage them in the KM measurement process. Let them assist in defining and aligning measures.

Ernst & Young measures KM in ways that its management wants to see. Consequently, its measures align with organizational goals, demonstrate improved performance, help manage risk, and show a clear ROI. The KM program presents high-level metrics that serve as an executive summary, as well as more detailed measurements that guide communities or practice in understanding how resources are being used, contributed to, and maintained. At the executive level, it provides a one-page dashboard showing the impact of various metrics linked to the organization's strategic goals. Detailed metrics track and monitor the granular components of each community, such as who uses the community Web site, how frequently they visit, how much content people contribute, and how current the content is. The KM program also obtains information from quarterly surveys and from feedback sessions focused on the awareness and perceived value of KM resources. The most enduring lessons in measuring KM follow.

- *Keep it simple.* People need to understand what it is that you are measuring and the intended use for the results.

- *Measure the use of knowledge.* This is typically more important than measuring participation or even impact.
- *Do not always wait until you have the perfect numbers to make business decisions.* Never underestimate the power of a good success story. Anecdotal success stories prove to be effective in gaining buy-in and support from senior management. Nor should you abdicate judgment and responsibility by asking for more data. Analysis paralysis is *not* a best practice.

Roles of KM Core Group

The KM core group's role in measurement is to:

- Examine any existing measures to see if they still provide accurate and meaningful information
- Articulate the benefits and risks associated with using an existing measure versus creating the ideal measure
- Create a process for collecting the measures from the business or functional units
- Assign business partners to monitor and report measures
- Analyze the impact of measures and report to management

Closing Comments

KM can produce amazing benefits, but if there are no measures and compelling results, then your entire program will falter. By starting with KM strategy and business objectives and analyzing knowledge gaps that impede those objectives, you will ensure your KM approaches and activities achieve measurable results.

And you get the best results by measuring the impact of KM from a program's inception. It leads to better design and better outcomes. Without a measurement system, management attention waivers, funds tend to dry up, and pleas for more money fall on deaf ears. KM programs get relegated to an afterthought, and KM core groups find themselves reassigned. The loss is unnecessary.

Those of us who understand the power of sharing knowledge must ensure we speak the language of the business and translate KM benefits into a measurable ROI. Knowledge in action can get results, be it better sales and selling approaches, by avoiding mistakes and rework, or by linking employees to expertise. If data proves that your employees are using and participating in KM approaches, then you know something of value is happening.

So measure what matters. Use measures that will improve your KM program. If data are collected just because they can be (by automated methods, for example), then your stakeholders could soon be overwhelmed or underimpressed. Instead, use the information in this chapter to ensure that KM approaches support your organizations' goals and are grounded by meaningful measures that lead to better outcomes and broader applications.

Implementation Resources

The following APQC resources can help you design measures and evaluate your KM program:

- APQC's KM Measurement Toolkit
- APQC's Standard KM Measures
- APQC's Measurement Alignment Worksheet
- Audio: *The Lost Measures: Cracking the Code*
- *Designing Measures for Knowledge Management*
- *Effective Measurement of Knowledge Management Initiatives: An APQC Overview*
- *Measurement in the 21st Century*
- *Measuring the Impact of Knowledge Management*

These resources—along with APQC's custom advisory services and more than 1,000 articles focused on KM—are available at www.apqc.org and through this book's Web site at www.newedgeinknowledge.com.

C H A P T E R

11

Make Best Practices Your Practices

The world has changed and KM is the beneficiary. Digital immersion makes people more comfortable with virtual work and virtual communities. The rise of mobile devices and decline in attention span force us to "be brief and be there" at the teachable moment. A changing of the guard as the baby boomers retire opens our organizations to new ways of thinking and collaborating.

Over the years, we have developed robust and repeatable KM approaches. The need and value of sharing knowledge are well accepted. People want to participate if you make it easy and in their flow. And the Enterprise 2.0 paradigm gives more people more control and input. Best of all, great organizations are willing to share how they make all of this work for them.

This chapter revisits some of our earlier themes in light of these successes and examples we have shared and highlights a few of the principles we think are important to take away, as well as suggesting how to get started.

Above and In the Flow

Throughout the book, we point out obvious and not-so-obvious ways to help embed KM in the flow of work. Let's review.

- *Know when to be in the flow.* Enabling employees to do their work more easily—by collaborating and capturing and sharing knowledge without an additional burden or interruption on their part—is doing KM *in* the work flow. Asking colleagues to stop their work process to move to another mode to reflect, capture, or share is doing KM *above* the work flow. Both have their place.

- *Form design teams and communities of practice around business and operational people.* We understand that it's not always easy to know what will thrive in your culture, especially when looking through a high-level, organization-wide lens. That's why we encourage you throughout this book to solicit input from all types of stakeholders and engage employees in the design of your KM approaches. People support what they help create, and they have an intuitive feel for what makes sense in your organization's culture. They will ensure KM supports their flow.

- *Be there at the teachable moment.* Ensure timely answers to questions and requests for help so that you don't break the flow of work. Being there at the teachable moment and speed of response is a direct predictor of satisfaction and participation in KM approaches. (There is nothing like instant gratification for increasing a behavior.) KM programs can use emerging 2.0 technologies to enable knowledge sharing at these teachable moments, with just enough detail, just in time, and just for that employee.

- *Use a standard collaboration platform across the enterprise.* People will be "doing KM" without knowing it, and you can design unobtrusive applications and add-ons to capture nuggets and knowledge from day-to-day interactions.

Other Principles

There are other principles that are worth mentioning before we leave.

- *Don't forget about the power of person to person and face to face.* We can get so caught up with saving travel time and dollars, and mesmerized with the latest virtual toy that we forget the value of face to face—the rich environment for creating and responding to teachable moments, discussing complex and sensitive topics, and creating lasting relationships.

- *Measurement matters.* Measures link KM to the *enduring* business value propositions identified in Chapter 2, be it helping an executive solve a central business model problem, innovating faster by connecting people, or reducing the cycle time to making an informed decision. This provides a way for your business leaders and stakeholders to begin to see the relationship between investments in KM approaches and their bottom-line results. Helping today wins you the right to help tomorrow.

From the moment you start looking for the KM value proposition, think about how you would measure impact. It will give you a laser-like focus on what matters to your organization's mission. It could change the whole direction of your KM strategy. And both you and KM become more valuable assets to your organization.

- *Create an enterprise KM strategy.* An enterprise KM strategy and program:
  - Creates a better user experience for employees who belong to multiple groups
  - Promotes efficient use of KM and IT resources
  - Increases the probability of standardization and reuse of content
  - Provides clarity around the business case and deliverables for approaches
  - Enables a focus on content and connectivity, instead of a specific KM approach
- *Link and leverage.* Build on what you already have in place or in play, from IT to strategic initiatives that are already getting a lot of attention. Reuse is a good thing for both the planet and for KM. This will reduce duplication of efforts, save money, and reduce the time necessary to design and implement common KM approaches.

Knowledge Resources

By analogy, link and leverage also applies to scarce knowledge resources such as technical or market expertise. You could centralize access to far flung and scarce experts rather than try to place them in every geography and project. For example, if you are interested in increasing your win rate on proposals, leveraging experts from across your organization to work on bids can ultimately increase your win rates while keeping costs low and cycle times short. Success doing that launched Schlumberger on its sustained KM trajectory.

So What Do You Do Monday Morning?

So, what is the first thing you should do? Complete APQC's KM Capability and Assessment Tool at www.newedgeinknowledge.com. You can take the abbreviated self-assessment on the Web site or you can contact APQC to engage in a deeper assessment and compare yourself to peer groups and specific best practices. Whether you are just getting started and have no formal KM program, you have long-standing KM approaches, or you are rebooting a stalled KM strategy, the results of this assessment will reveal your strengths and weaknesses and show you what you need to do next.

Your KM program will demand a lot. You will need stamina and persistence, steadfast conviction of your beliefs on what will work and the courage to say so, and change management and communication skills so employees will listen.

Turning individual knowledge into organizational knowledge is not for sissies. Without the right strategy, the right sponsors, and adequate funding (volunteers and heroic acts will take you only so far), you won't be able to achieve the profound good that comes to people and organizations that cherish, grow, and share knowledge.

But you don't have to do it alone.

Thousands of organizations have embraced KM, and you don't need to struggle for the right answers alone. KM professionals turn to APQC to connect to a worldwide community of peers from all industries and to gain exposure to ready-to-use knowledge. Networking opportunities include monthly Web events, an annual KM conference and training series, benchmarking research groups, advanced working groups, and access to a network of experts to answer your most pressing issues in KM. Join our community of KM professionals to work smarter and faster while making your KM practices go from good to great.

For implementation resources, access to pertinent benchmarks, helpful assessments, and more, you can start at our Web site at www.newedgeinknowledge.com or go directly to www.apqc.org. (Throughout the book, we detail the specific implementation resources and road maps, presentations, training, assessment tools, and articles that will help you further explore each chapter's topic.) We can point you in the right direction, whether you just want to see what other KM professionals are doing and doing well or you need a major implementation toolkit for a specific KM approach.

We had fun writing this book because we got to talk, bat ideas around, peel back layers, learn, explain, and share insights. That's what makes KM fun. Come to one of our conferences, join an APQC KM consortium, or give APQC a call. It's time to make best practices your practices. Let's have some fun.

Implementation Resources

The following APQC resources can help you implement a successful enterprise KM program:

- *Capturing Critical Knowledge from a Shifting Work Force*
- *Communities of Practice and Associations*
- *If Only We Knew What We Know: The Transfer of Internal Knowledge and Best Practice*
- *Knowledge Mapping: The Essentials for Success*
- *The Executive's Role in Knowledge Management*
- *Where Are You Now? A KM Program Self-Assessment*

These resources—along with APQC's custom advisory services and more than 1,000 articles focused on KM—are available at www.apqc.org and through this book's Web site at www.newedgeinknowledge.com.

Appendix: Case Studies

Throughout the book, we have shared best-practice examples from ConocoPhillips, Fluor, IBM, and MITRE. Let's now take a closer look at their KM programs and approaches. These cases are compelling illustrations of the KM principles we share throughout the book. They also provide a sense of how the principles can look very different in practice, when customized to fit a particular culture and business model. We applaud each of these organizations for making KM fit.

ConocoPhillips

ConocoPhillips is an international, integrated energy company and the third-largest oil and gas company in the United States. Based in Houston, the company is engaged in petroleum exploration and production; petroleum refining, marketing, and transportation; natural gas gathering, marketing, supply, and transportation; and chemicals and plastics production and distribution. ConocoPhillips is known for its technological expertise in areas such as reservoir management and exploration, 3D seismic technology, high-grade petroleum coke upgrading, and sulfur removal. Its nearly 30,000 employees are located across 30 countries.

The organization has a diverse heritage. Since the late 1990s, ConocoPhillips has grown through strategic transactions of various types involving more than 10 companies. Many of the transactions included dispersed and hard-to-reach areas around the world. Connecting people became a critical business objective for the organization. Knowledge-sharing methods were adapted to promote functional excellence and leverage knowledge across the organization. Knowledge-sharing sponsorship is now organization-wide and supported by all business streams. Specifically, knowledge sharing at ConocoPhillips is supported by the following business lines:

- Exploration and production (upstream)
- Project development and procurement
- Commercial
- Refining and marketing (downstream)
- Technology
- IT

An organization-wide knowledge-sharing function (i.e., KM core group) helps the organization achieve business goals through value-based, world-class, and organization-wide collaborative solutions and services. The ConocoPhillips knowledge-sharing vision is to become "a workplace where employees continuously deliver additional value through global collaboration and expertise sharing."

ConocoPhillips's knowledge-sharing strategy involves two primary elements: empowering others and building the network. The key to both is trust, which is the foundation for the organization's knowledge-sharing motto, FAST:

- *Find.* The ability to locate trusted, validated knowledge content when it is needed.
- *Ask colleagues.* Peer-to-peer problem solving through discussion forums and similar mechanisms.
- *Share expertise.* Expertise location functionality.
- *Trust.* Strong, global relationships that employees can depend on.

Finding content, asking colleagues, and sharing with experts enhance the ability to collaborate, learn, and maximize value. This is also how employees are trained to use network portal sites.

History of KM and Networks of Excellence

At ConocoPhillips, communities of practice are known as networks of excellence. Although networks have existed informally (and formally in a few cases) for more than 20 years, the first formalized, new-generation networks emerged in February 2005. As part of that deployment, a mixture of existing upstream and downstream communities were leveraged into official networks with global access. Throughout the journey, achieving functional excellence has been the foundational focus of networks. An upstream network model provided structure to networks. Communication strategies and training were added in 2007 to sustain and expand the effort.

Today, more than 120 networks exist across the organization. Networks align with business functions to assist in the achievement of functional excellence. The portals are open, in that both contract and full-time employees have access to most network activity. Given that between 70 percent and 80 percent of organizational learning occurs informally and outside the classroom, networks support informal learning among members.

Networks exist across all technical disciplines, and most are supported by functional excellence teams. Functional excellence teams include line managers from business units and assets who are accountable for networks. Functional excellence teams provide structure, governance, and leadership required for effective networks of excellence.

The knowledge-sharing leadership team (i.e., not the core group) includes representatives from various business streams across the organization who help set direction and strategy. The knowledge-sharing leadership team also provides support for reward and recognition programs organization-wide.

The enterprise knowledge-sharing team oversees network activities. Knowledge sharing is promoted through the use of Ask and Discuss forums and knowledge libraries, as well as a wiki. Discussion forums and knowledge libraries are embedded in each community portal. Network portals are accessed frequently; for example, ConocoPhillips recorded more than 1.3 million hits monthly on its family of SharePoint-based network portal sites during a six-month period between April and October 2009.

Within each community, the Ask and Discuss forum is a place to post questions and initiate discussions. The organization tracks the number of questions posted, the number of replies, and the number of readers per question or discussion. Data show that an average of 20 people read a single reply. In other words, for just five replies, about 100 people read the responses and absorb the information contained therein.

Content that complements Ask and Discuss forums is stored in the network's knowledge library. This content is reviewed and analyzed by subject matter experts and then posted to the library using a taxonomy developed by the knowledge-sharing team and corroborated by network leaders. Knowledge library content is quality controlled; only the most valuable knowledge is retained in the library.

Networks of Excellence Approach

ConocoPhillips's networks are based on a network building blocks model, which identifies 10 critical success factors for creating and sustaining networks:

1. Leadership and sponsorship
2. A clear business case
3. Adequate resources and defined roles
4. Member engagement
5. Deliverables and activities
6. The development of trusted relationships
7. Knowledge transfer processes
8. Supporting technology
9. Rewards, recognition, and motivation
10. Network measurements

Networks must address each of the building blocks to ensure success. If one of the blocks is missing or weak, then the network runs the risk of collapse.

The first building block, leadership and sponsorship, is vital to network success. As Dan Ranta, ConocoPhillips's knowledge-sharing director, said: "Grassroots initiatives are fine, but can only go so far without leadership support. Networks need management to set direction and strategy."

The second building block, establishing a clear business case, is important because it helps attract leadership support. A network's business case must provide defined objectives that affect operational excellence or result in business improvements. Before a launch, with the help of a standardized template, networks outline a business case that clearly articulates business value and deliverables. Examples of deliverables include cost reductions and reductions in capital expenditures. Networks identify business impact and define a value proposition, key activities, deliverables, and measures of success. The business case is updated throughout the network's life cycle.

Outlining key resources, roles, and expectations is another critical success factor for sustaining networks. ConocoPhillips's Network

University is an online resource that provides standard role descriptions for network support positions, including sponsors or leaders, core team members, subject matter experts, and network members. Available documents list the types of activities and behaviors required for each role, and users can download descriptions and best-practice examples.

Articulating how networks retain corporate knowledge also helps attract network sponsorship. Figure A.1 depicts the components of ConocoPhillips's knowledge retention strategy.

Governance

ConocoPhillips's knowledge-sharing team (i.e., the KM core group) is responsible for overseeing the organization's 120-plus networks of excellence. Formed in 2006 and comprising six full-time individuals, the knowledge-sharing team is embedded in the corporate planning and strategy function. The team addresses strategic goals and leverages resources across the organization. Working with all business streams and functional units, it is responsible for maintaining established networks and managing associated training, metrics, and portal sites.

Figure A.1   Knowledge Retention Model at ConocoPhillips

The knowledge-sharing leadership team (which is different from the core group) sets direction and strategy for knowledge-sharing initiatives, including networks of excellence. Knowledge-sharing leadership team members are key leaders from across the enterprise. The knowledge-sharing leadership team is critical and was built one person at a time. The organization found individuals in geographically dispersed locations who were passionate about sharing knowledge and willing to serve in a leadership capacity. In addition to setting strategy, the team selects top business units and regions for knowledge-sharing recognition, as well as the top networks and the success stories of the year.

Within networks, a core leadership team guides specific network activities. Each network typically has 8 to 15 core team leaders who manage the network. The key is to engage people with passion to serve as core team members. By becoming focal points for their locations or regions within the networks, these individuals facilitate vital face-to-face interaction among network members. Core team members rotate positions and receive coaching from the knowledge-sharing team on how to lead and engage networks.

Funding

Funding for networks is allocated to business streams. Some networks receive seed money to get started, but funding is expected to be distributed eventually across business units. Networks benefit the bottom line; business units realize this and are willing to allocate funds to ensure that networks are successful.

The knowledge-sharing team has a budget for technology platforms; however, costs associated with network leaders, sponsors, and core team members are allocated to the business units. Each network must complete a business case that outlines resource allocations, and the relevant business unit must approve resources before any network launch.

Practices for Promoting and Sustaining Participation

Building a collaborative culture was part of the ConocoPhillips strategy. Changing the mind-set of employees was imperative; the organization didn't want knowledge sharing to be viewed as another initiative that required additional time or resources. A senior executive helped communicate the value and purpose of global knowledge sharing, and the knowledge-sharing team worked to convince others of the urgency for networks and the value of connecting people. "We were less concerned about content at first," Ranta said. "It was really about connecting people and sharing lessons learned." Eventually, linking network performance to the remuneration structure helped further promote the use of networks.

Developing trusting relationships among members is a network imperative. "We need to cultivate online trust," Ranta said. "Otherwise, people go down the hall to the person they've known for 20 years when they have a question."

To build trust, the organization promotes face-to-face meetings and networking. Its annual Network Leadership Summit, for example, brings together network leaders to share lessons learned and encourages networking. About 70 percent of community leaders are located at the Houston headquarters. In 2009, some sessions were made virtual for leaders outside of Houston who were unable to attend in person. The summit helps leaders develop stronger relationships, which ultimately improves connections and content in networks.

Promoting intracommunity collaboration is a strategy designed to help transfer lessons learned. Networks can communicate to an entire membership or a targeted audience using portal functionality to push content out. The ability to connect cross-stream networks is valuable; it helps promote collaboration across business sectors, where appropriate.

The organization's new collaboration tool, OneWiki, will further tie together external content, success stories, lessons learned, and reference documents, including closed discussion items. Once fully implemented, OneWiki will ensure that everyone has access to knowledge in one place. The knowledge library stores approved content, which can be accessed using links in OneWiki.

The wiki approach could mitigate barriers to knowledge sharing by empowering newer employees to conduct basic research before consulting a subject matter expert. Wikis also are expected to further engage core teams, subject matter experts, and new employees who will be working in tandem to develop wiki articles. Controlling the quantity of wiki content is considered manageable because, according to Network Specialist Miriam Fjellaker, "Research shows that 90 percent of wiki users read, 9 percent make edits, and only 1 percent add new wiki articles."

Challenges

Baby boomers nearing retirement age pose a challenge to sustaining effective networks. At ConocoPhillips, nearly 20 percent of the employee base is eligible for retirement. In the coming years, another nearly 20 percent will qualify for retirement. These highly experienced employees possess valuable business knowledge and often serve as subject matter experts or network leaders. It is vital to capture their knowledge and experience so that it can be reused across the enterprise and accelerate learning.

Losing core team network members presents another challenge to networks of excellence. The project management network, for example, frequently redeploys and reassigns network leaders and core team members in the organization. High leadership turnover rates can lead to network disengagement and a loss of expertise. The knowledge-sharing team works closely with networks that experience changes in leadership to overcome obstacles and find ways to sustain continuous leadership.

Keeping Networks Vital   Each network leader establishes network goals. Goals are outlined in the business case and clearly articulated to the network members. Reward and recognition programs are also designed to keep networks of excellence vital across the organization.

Member Engagement   When ConocoPhillips first began launching networks, business units perceived them as a corporate initiative that was being added to normal workloads (i.e., above the flow of work). Membership engagement has helped change that perception and is one of the building blocks required for successful networks of excellence.

Creating connections between similar networks increases engagement and allows the organization to leverage knowledge more effectively. Sister networks are linked by business objectives and functions. One network currently has 16 sister networks. Network members can post Ask and Discuss questions to related networks to engage a broader audience in finding a solution. Only meaningful, out-of-the-ordinary questions approved by the network leader are posted to sister network sites. The goal is to further engage similar networks and let others know of network issues and activities.

Network leaders are constantly aware of the need to promote engagement and increase membership. One method for promoting engagement is to transition members from e-mail to the knowledge portal to more effectively drive use of the Ask and Discuss forums. When a leader receives an e-mail message, for example, he or she may suggest that the member post the question on the network portal; this action will encourage users to become more active in the network by visiting the site rather than posting a question to a single resource. Network leaders also drive network participation by posting new announcements, events, and discussion items in the portal. Keeping the network fresh helps sustain members' interest.

Another strategy for member engagement involves incorporating network use into day-to-day job responsibilities. Deliberately designing the network through business planning makes activities more relevant to individuals; the intersection between network activities and daily business functions is expanding. The goal is to link part of an individual's performance expectations to network participation, which boosts engagement as well as knowledge sharing.

Employee growth and development is also linked to network activities, which helps promote member engagement. For example, career development strategies highlight the use of networks as a way to grow professionally in the organization.

Global Networks   All 120-plus networks are global, and this can present some challenges. The knowledge-sharing team works with the network leaders and network core teams to address these challenges as they arise.

One such challenge is the cultural differences among various regions with regard to sharing knowledge. Whereas most Westerners are fairly comfortable with posting questions and comments to Ask and Discuss forums, engaging members in the Asia-Pacific region can be more difficult because employees from these cultures are less comfortable singling out individuals. Core team members in these regions work diligently to build network participation.

Time zones present another challenge for global networks. Virtual meetings are scheduled in the early morning or the evening to accommodate different parts of the world and can be repeated at 12-hour intervals if needed.

Roles

Several hundred employees across ConocoPhillips work on knowledge-sharing activities, most of them part-time. As mentioned, the core knowledge-sharing team supports network activities, and six full-time resources help manage networks. Each network is supported by a network sponsor and leader, a core team, network members, and subject matter experts.

Network Sponsors   A network sponsor provides overall guidance and visibility for the network. Sponsors are influential senior-level managers from organization-wide business streams. They secure funding and help set direction and strategy with community leaders.

A network sponsor also helps create and refine the network's business case and verify buy-in with business unit leaders. He or she supports the network through executive briefings and communication with stakeholders. Sponsors appoint, coach, and support network leaders, including linking their performance to career progression. In addition, sponsors ensure that network members' community activities are recognized and rewarded within their business units and globally.

Network Leaders   Networks of excellence are supported by network leaders who are selected by sponsors or business-unit leaders. These individuals are responsible for ensuring that core team members, subject matter experts, and other network members understand the purpose of the community and their roles and responsibilities. They work closely with the network sponsors to ensure that the focus of the network reflects business unit needs. Network leaders also seek feedback from core team members about network activity, communicate the value of participation, and solicit business unit feedback.

In addition to checking the community portal for submissions and pushing new content to members and subject matter experts, leaders:

- Facilitate responses for portal-based questions in a timely manner
- Direct Ask and Discuss questions to the appropriate subject matter expert or member
- Encourage the regular use of content with questions

Leaders help train members on how to use the tools and resources available in the community. They also acknowledge member participation with awards, recognition, and performance feedback.

The time spent on leadership activities varies by network. One individual may manage three networks and spend approximately 33 percent of his or her time doing this. Others may spend 20 percent of their time on managing one network, depending on other business demands. The role is integrated with job responsibilities; it is not an additional role that leaders are expected to assume on top of their day-to-day functions. "They don't put on another hat and stop doing their other jobs," said Miriam Fjellaker, network specialist. "The role is integrated and helps them improve their other job functions."

Core Team Members   Core team members check the portal site daily for new submissions and developments and respond to Ask and Discuss questions. They also set up alerts for members on key content areas. Core team members also:

- Work with network leaders and sponsors to make sure the needs and issues of the local business unit are adequately reflected within the scope and activities of the global network
- Push e-mail threads to the portal as much as possible
- Communicate community activities to the business unit
- Empower and encourage members to use networks as part of their daily work processes

Network Members   Network members are encouraged to select and join the networks that relate to their work. They are also encouraged to share knowledge, best practices, and lessons learned in the network portal and leverage network relationships to ask questions, get answers, and learn with global colleagues.

Subject Matter Experts   Subject matter experts share knowledge, best practices, and lessons learned in the network portal. They also work with the community and other subject matter experts to develop and agree on best practices. Being responsive is important; subject matter experts are encouraged to respond to Ask and Discuss questions related to their areas of expertise as quickly as possible. They are expected to use their expertise to move others forward. Subject matter experts also provide input to the network leader and core team regarding how their areas of expertise should be addressed in the network's business case and other projects and initiatives.

Technology for Networks

SharePoint is used across the enterprise to post questions and promote knowledge sharing. A dedicated team creates and manages portal sites and networks. All networks are standardized and have the same look and feel. "We say it's not about technology; but without it, we couldn't do what we do today," said Murray Smith, coordinator of the organization's floating production systems network.

Cultural Enablers for Sustaining Networks

Networks at ConocoPhillips vary in size, scope, and function. The goal, said Smith, is to uncover the unique personality of each network and promote a culture that works. "You can't click your heels and change the culture; leaders have to make it happen."

The community leader is expected to brainstorm ways to shape the culture and increase engagement. Pushing alerts and responding to Ask and Discuss questions are important and help promote a culture that is conducive to sharing knowledge.

Knowledge sharing is indirectly linked to ConocoPhillips's performance and incentive compensation structure. This link serves as a strong motivator for employees to participate in knowledge sharing, and it demonstrates the organizational commitment to networks of excellence.

Reward and recognition programs are designed to increase network participation. Specifically, a reward and recognition structure helps motivate employees to participate in networks and promotes a knowledge-sharing culture. Training is another cultural enabler. ConocoPhillips has a number of training efforts that explain network functionality and potential.

Training   The Network University is the training vehicle that supports ConocoPhillips's network activities from launch to deployment. Network University provides access to documents, presentations, and role descriptions that help form and maintain networks. Quick links from the KM home page provide overviews for new and experienced members. Users can also download a FAQ on networks or link to established sites.

The organization uses Network University to train network leaders. It provides detailed descriptions of roles and expectations related to network leadership. The more than 150 network leaders frequently go to the site for guidance on how to maintain networks at ConocoPhillips. In addition, less experienced network leaders are often paired with experienced leaders for mentoring purposes.

New hires receive training on networks during the onboarding process. A 90-minute segment shows how to map to networks and how networks tap in to expertise across the organization to better share knowledge.

Communication   Communicating the value and purpose of networks of excellence is critical to sustaining engagement and attracting new members. According to Ranta, "We realized we had to get out there and tell our story if we wanted networks to succeed."

The organization continues to increase communication efforts designed to spread the word on the value of networks. Network leaders and sponsors frequently communicate success stories to network members.

External validation is promoted across the organization. For example, a number of corporate magazine articles showcase the success of networks at ConocoPhillips. The organization publicizes these articles to show the value of network activity. In 2009, ConocoPhillips was named a North American Most Admired Knowledge Enterprise (MAKE), and this award was also communicated across the organization.

Communication is so important to the overall success of ConocoPhillips's knowledge-sharing program that one of its full-time knowledge-sharing team members, Yvonne Myles, is the designated communications adviser. This individual supports the communication efforts of the networks of excellence along with communication initiatives that promote networks to the larger organization and externally.

Each network uses a portal to communicate activities and news. In addition to linking to key news and discussions, portals showcase award recipients and network leaders.

Participation Recognition   Motivating employees to participate in networks of excellence is critical. Global and local rewards programs recognize members for network participation. For example, the prestigious Archimedes Award is presented to the top networks and success stories each year and recognizes regions for their knowledge-sharing behaviors.

ConocoPhillips also collects collaboration success stories to high-light the business value of networks. To date, there are thousands of success stories that provide optimal business solutions. The stories are quality controlled and stored in the knowledge repository for future access.

The global awards program recognizes contributions to the organization by using the four Gs—give, grab, gather, and guts—through which award recipients are selected on the basis of their ability to give, grab, and gather knowledge. The *guts* piece pertains to the ability to share painful lessons learned.

Regional areas sometimes create their own awards. Other recognition programs are supported by peers and implemented across networks.

Peers may also nominate members for awards through the network portal. Online submission is quick and easy. Members are nominated for excellence in contributions, Ask and Discuss forum participation, and engaging others in trusted relationships. Some networks of excellence have an award for outstanding discussions. Winners are celebrated on the network home page.

Measuring Networks of Excellence

ConocoPhillips's knowledge-sharing team employs both objective and subjective tools to evaluate the health of the organization's networks, identify where weaknesses exist, and prescribe ways for network leaders to improve their networks. Measuring the business impact of networks is a regular activity for the knowledge-sharing team and network leaders.

Assessing Networks for Value: Success Stories   ConocoPhillips believes that "you manage what you measure." Keeping detailed records of business impact has served to galvanize sponsorship and attract and sustain membership to networks. One way the organization assesses business value is through validated success stories. Stories are submitted by employees and document cost savings, reduced cycle times, safety and environmental improvements, and other tangible business benefits. A story may also identify a critical business or technical issue that was solved using the community. Each year, the organization collects success story nominations and selects the best examples of collaboration.

Supervisors, regional representatives, and the knowledge-sharing leadership team review and validate each story, adding a value statement to provide a quick snapshot of the business value provided. Once success stories are approved, they are posted to the knowledge library where they can be accessed by other networks. To date, more than 5,000 success stories have been captured in the knowledge library. The overall business impact from KM measured in the hundreds of millions of dollars from 2005 to 2010.

Assessing Network Health   Many networks of excellence participate in a network diagnostic process with the knowledge-sharing team. Leaders and sponsors evaluate network health against the 10 aforementioned critical building blocks. Some network diagnostics occur every six months, whereas others are conducted annually. Each of the critical success factors has a set of criteria associated with it; for example, the section on member engagement reviews member growth, member contributions, and subject matter expert participation. Once leaders review the criteria and identify areas for improvement, the knowledge-sharing team helps the network identify enhancement strategies. The knowledge-sharing team maintains reports that summarize the health of each network.

Portal audits review the content and functionality of portals to ensure they function effectively for end users. Content is reviewed to make sure it is up to date, and functionality is tested to make sure the site functions as intended. Using a 1 to 10 rating scale, knowledge-sharing team members rank the effectiveness of the home page, the Ask and Discuss forum, processes for finding and submitting content, membership processes, and work groups. A detailed summary review provides recommendations and considerations, as well as action items.

The knowledge-sharing team uses standard metrics to evaluate the level of collaboration occurring within the networks. These metrics evaluate collaboration related to Ask and Discuss participation as well as overall readership. Leaders can identify who participates frequently and who rarely visits the network. A leader might provide a gentle push to users who are reading information and suggest they sign up to receive alerts on a related area of interest.

Quarterly collaboration metrics also identify:

- Total network participants
- Contributions from nonmembers
- Individuals who read in the portal but do not contribute or sign up as members
- Members who read but do not post in Ask and Discuss
- Individuals who are fully immersed and actively read and contribute

Each category is presented with a potential opportunity for improvement. For example, nonmembers who contribute may be contacted to join a network, since they are already participating. Similarly, individuals who read posts might be encouraged to join. Members who frequently read Ask and Discuss questions may be encouraged to share what they know by more actively participating in networks. Finally, members who are fully immersed in the network are encouraged to become knowledge brokers and recruit new members.

Network maturity is also reviewed by the knowledge-sharing team. There are six levels of network maturity.

Level One represents a basic network with active membership.
Level Two networks share content with sister networks and obtain quantifiable business results.
Level Three networks incorporate functional areas that affect the network.
Level Four networks include vertical functions in opportunities to connect with people.
Level Five networks include joint ventures. For example, a question from a joint venture in Malaysia can tap into technical areas for answers to project delivery and management issues.
Level Six networks incorporate external knowledge-sharing strategies.

Maintaining Alignment with Business Processes   By design, knowledge sharing is aligned with the business processes at ConocoPhillips. Organization-wide leadership applies a formal network governance structure across all business streams. Functional leadership provides the structure, governance, and leadership necessary for effective networks. Functional excellence teams are accountable for networks.

Fluor

Fluor Corporation is one of the world's largest publicly traded engineering, procurement, construction, maintenance, and project management organizations. It was founded as a construction company in 1912. Today, the organization develops and implements solutions in diverse industries, including chemicals and petrochemicals, government services, life sciences, manufacturing, mining, oil and gas, telecommunications, and transportation infrastructure.

Its projects include designing and building manufacturing facilities, refineries, pharmaceutical facilities, health care buildings, power plants, and telecommunications and transportation infrastructure. Fluor also provides operations and maintenance services for its projects, as well as administrative and support services to the U.S. government. Fluor maintains a network of offices in more than 25 countries across six continents.

Fluor's business environment is global, mobile, cyclical, and collaborative. Employees are located across the globe and must work together closely for distributed project execution. Workforce scarcity and mobility is a reality at Fluor; finding experts around the world is critical to its business environment. Also, because of the organization's aging workforce, knowledge retention is an increasingly important issue. The business environment also requires supply chain integration and collaboration, since many of Fluor's projects involve multiparty project execution.

History of KM and Knowledge Communities

For more than 20 years, Fluor informally used KM strategies and techniques to enhance collaboration and leverage collective knowledge. In 1999, the organization implemented a formal KM program to promote a consistent KM strategy across the organization. The CEO's mandate was to "transform Fluor into the premier knowledge-based services company."

When Fluor launched its organization-wide KM effort, its vision was to have one technology solution that included communities with integrated content, discussions, and people profiles to help it promote a global mind-set. Leveraging the collective intellectual capital of all employees to support business strategic direction was a key objective. Communities were designed to provide optimal solutions by promoting knowledge across geographic and business-line boundaries, offering a robust search capability, and allowing global access. Organization-wide KM was also targeted to enhance employee skill sets by giving them easy access to knowledge and training materials and by connecting them to expertise. Finally, organization-wide KM protects intellectual property in the organization. Fluor's KM system monitors downloads to safeguard intellectual property.

Today, Fluor has 46 established knowledge communities; 24,000 active community members; and more than 3,500 subject matter experts in 1,000-plus subject areas. Virtually 100 percent of Fluor's professional staff is active in the knowledge communities. The volume of community activity is high, with more than 10,000 searches daily, 2,600 attachment views or downloads daily, and 10,000 forum reads on a weekly basis.

At Fluor, communities are about people, and this belief is continuously communicated across the organization. "We really emphasize that communities are where we work and live," said John McQuary, vice president of KM and technology strategies. "Communities are more than just a place to find knowledge; they are support systems where employees can obtain a sense of belonging and enrich their skill sets and careers."

Beyond a simple technology implementation, a successful knowledge community needs:

- People
- Strong local support
- To invest in itself
- To coexist with its environment
- The culture to enrich the lives of its people

Every employee has access to all knowledge communities, even if the individual is not a community member. Fluor uses a push model for community communications. In other words, when an employee joins a community, he or she begins receiving e-mails, newsletters, and updates. The individual must be a member of the community to be identified as a community expert or knowledge reviewer.

For the most part, knowledge communities at Fluor are aligned by functional processes and business lines. The functional communities are built on the platform of Fluor's functional excellence networks, some of which have existed for more than 20 years. In fact, 18 of the 46 communities represent functional networks or processes; project management, electrical engineering, and construction are three examples of global functional networks.

Figure A.2 depicts Fluor's community alignment model. Business-line communities are organized by key business industries. Corporate communities cut across business lines and include functions such as HR, IT, and finance. Strategic initiative communities are designed on an as-needed basis to address strategic corporate initiatives. For example, the organization created a specialized community to address next-generation technology needs.

The functional communities leverage Fluor's project excellence networks, which represent every function that is staffed on projects or programs (e.g., project management, project controls, and estimating). Each of the 18 functional communities is led by a global excellence leader, and this individual is considered the highest authority within the organization on that function or discipline. For example, the mechanical engineer who is assigned as the global excellence leader is the highest-authority mechanical engineer in the organization.

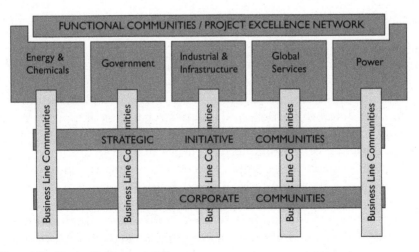

Figure A.2   Community Alignment at Fluor

Global excellence leaders develop and maintain functional networks (i.e., communities) that cross all business groups. They provide leadership for their respective knowledge communities. Specifically, global excellence leaders are responsible for best-practice approvals, reference systems, and career paths for the organization, including training, required readings, and unique tools for that discipline. An additional responsibility is career development. The role is prestigious; after serving as global excellence leaders, many individuals become Fluor executives.

Communities are supported by leaders, knowledge managers, a global core KM team, and subject matter experts. A centralized KM team oversees community activities and works closely with leaders, knowledge managers, and subject matter experts across the enterprise.

Knowledge OnLine is Fluor's centralized digital hub for all knowledge sharing activities, resources, and intellectual property. It is accessed through the corporate portal. Within Knowledge OnLine, subject matter experts and community members maintain profiles that showcase their expertise. Each profile includes a member picture and incorporates technical background and project industry experience. Members attach current résumés to their profiles. "We ask our experts to perform a search on their expertise to make sure they show up in the search results," McQuary said. "This gives experts ideas on what they need to highlight in their profiles."

Strategy for Sustaining Effective Networks of Excellence

Fluor is a good example of what it means to have an enterprise KM strategy and program. Fluor's KM program replicates its community, content, discussions, and profiling approaches across its 42 functional and four corporate communities. It implies a global mind-set, with consistency of purpose and practice regardless of topic or geography. It implies designing KM so that each employee can tap in to the knowledge of the organization as a whole in order to respond to a client's needs. It also implies access to content and people from anywhere clients or employees need help to solve a problem or enhance their skill.

Knowledge communities are used to drive organizational transformation. In fact, communities are often created to fill a business need or knowledge gap and then decommissioned when they are no longer relevant. A work-share community, for example, addressed practices and procedures that were required to work in New Delhi and Manila. Now these practices are embedded into daily work processes and incorporated into standard operating procedures, and the community no longer exists. Similarly, a next-generation community is currently in place to explore future technology solutions. However, when next-generation technology is implemented and begins to become the de facto way to work, this community's content will be migrated into appropriate mainstream communities for long-term stewardship.

Communities also provide work process innovation. For example, practice and procedure updates are managed and implemented in communities. A subject matter expert uses a discussion forum to collect suggestions or ideas to improve a procedure document. Using feedback from community members, the subject matter expert will update a policy or procedure and review changes. This process helps gain buy-in for policy and procedure changes, as well as global buy-in for the practice. The approach also has an associated cost benefit. "In the past, we had large budgets for this process. Today, we set a goal of updating or reviewing one-third of the practices using a fraction of the old budget," McQuary said.

Communities also support more distributed project execution at Fluor. The organization uses a project activity model to illustrate activities and provide project management guidance. Using the community framework, members are able to update a map and provide color-coded areas of responsibility for more effective project execution. Communities can add training materials on how to complete project activities, along with templates and descriptions.

Another work process improvement is linked to the organizational communication strategy. The old practice was to disseminate information about communities through the organizational hierarchy. However, not everyone saw those communications. Now, communities send newsletters to the entire community membership. As a result, messages have a broader readership (greater penetration), which ultimately helps attract new members. Each message is sent as an e-mail with a link to the latest newsletter. This draws in employees who perhaps are not familiar with the system, thereby potentially recruiting new members. Employees frequently reply to messages and are encouraged to join a particular community as part of a routine follow-up.

Knowledge Loss Risk Assessment

Communities help in the identification of knowledge gaps or knowledge at risk—that is, knowledge that might be lost if the individual who possesses it retires from the organization. Fluor uses a knowledge-loss risk assessment process to determine the impact of retirement and resource gaps. The assessments also effectively communicate the potential impact of knowledge loss. Adapted from the Tennessee Valley Authority model, the formula multiplies the retirement factor (how soon) against the position risk factor (uniqueness of the individual's knowledge) to determine the total attrition factor. This process helps integrate knowledge sharing with human capital management by identifying when subject matter expertise is at risk and when the organization should identify a successor or protégé for a subject matter expert.

Governance

Fluor's global core KM team consists of eight full-time equivalent (FTE) employees who are responsible for community activities and management. Responsibilities are segmented by communications, operations, community coordination, and Knowledge OnLine. In reality, however, the team works across functions to address KM needs. The team is supported by a KM network that includes community leaders, knowledge managers, and KM champions—local advocates spread across Fluor's global offices.

As the KM program has matured, the core KM team has adjusted its role accordingly. Fluor's community journey officially began with the launch of two pilot communities in 1999. The pilots validated the community deployment process and underlying technology. During the first community rollouts, the team focused on reaching high-volume community targets. About 30 communities were quickly formed, but about half failed due to improper organizational alignment. The team then adjusted its community emphasis to focus on performance. The performance-based approach eventually evolved to sustained performance to communicate the corporate commitment to communities and their value to the organization.

Today, the core KM team operates on the principle of instinctive performance. The team works closely with business leaders and relies on the collective expertise of the KM team to help drive strategic direction and activities. "We don't necessarily wait for executives to tell us what to do, yet everything we do must support the business strategy," said Dan Nerison, manager, Fluor KM team.

Funding

The KM team receives organizational funding for labor, expenses, Knowledge OnLine, and external software. This budget is allocated out to the businesses. Functional communities and networks are provided with a budget for functional management, people development, standards and procedures, and specific initiatives. Knowledge managers are also funded for services they provide to functional networks.

Practices for Promoting and Sustaining Community Activity

Promoting knowledge communities across the community life cycle, from initial deployment to sustained performance, is a defined business strategy at Fluor.

Community growth and development are sustained and nurtured through charter creation, launch, deployment, and performance maintenance. The achievement of initial community objectives is assessed a few months after deployment. Performance is evaluated by examining the quality and quantity of forum and discussion activity, business alignment, and achievement of stated objectives.

Community Deployment   The community deployment process is rigorous and consistent. Each community must complete a readiness assessment based on specific criteria that evaluate whether it is aligned with business objectives and strategy. For example, each community must:

- Align with overall objectives, goals, and business relevance
- Align with principles of knowledge sharing
- Obtain sponsorship
- Identify available and committed resources
- Understand KM deployment process, costs, and benefits
- Commit to required behavior changes
- Meet a high-priority business demand

Once community readiness is determined, community leaders begin a series of deployment workshops. These workshops, which take a minimum of three months to complete, focus on identifying leadership teams, outlining community structures, and collecting content. Content must be comprehensive and useful to ensure that members find value in the community immediately after launch.

Fluor has an explicit process for community deployment and performance. Once content is identified, collected, and organized, a launch strategy is developed with input from the KM team. Following the launch, workshops focus on performance to sustain engagement. Ongoing performance meetings ensure that the community continues to perform as expected and provide business value.

Fluor's core KM team rarely decommissions a community. Because the process for creating, deploying, and sustaining a community is rigorous and thorough, most communities continue to perform. The KM core team also diligently measures community performance and works closely with community leaders if a community appears to be faltering. If participation declines after deployment, then the team intervenes to ensure effective leadership.

Challenges to Sustaining Communities Avoiding the community performance blues is important at Fluor. Community health is in jeopardy if a community demonstrates a loss of momentum and attention. Discontinued communications, lack of leadership, or undefined or unachievable objectives often contribute to a decline in momentum. Likewise, time allocation, workload, and prioritization may result in a loss of attention. Also, when communities are localized and dominated by a host office or small core of engaged members, they are not likely to provide value. The core team looks for these indicators when assessing overall community health and works closely with communities to determine whether performance is declining.

Predictors of Success Effective knowledge leadership is the leading predictor of success for Fluor's communities. Knowledge leaders communicate openly and frequently with communities and are visible role models of desired behaviors. Community leaders recognize that they are helping to create a knowledge-sharing culture and facilitate people-to-people connections. Leaders also make sure it is safe for employees to ask questions, share openly, and trust the answers they receive.

In addition, knowledge leaders recognize that a community is a human community, not a technology implementation. Leaders understand that they are responsible for the human capital component of their communities and encourage lifelong learning.

It is also important that knowledge leaders acknowledge the talent and intelligence within the organization. Leaders inspire community members to combine experience and innovative thinking to create new knowledge, and they encourage the community to work smarter through collaboration. Finally, leaders connect the community with strategic direction and drive for business results. They know that greater energy is available when people are connected through a sense of purpose.

Keeping Communities Vital   One way that Fluor keeps communities vital is by updating content on a regular basis. The organization implemented processes to ensure that communities frequently review and revise content. Each community is expected to take responsibility for its intellectual assets. Submitted content must be looked over and assigned a future review date prior to approval. Each community is assigned a knowledge manager with domain expertise who manages community content by accepting, rejecting, or forwarding content for review. The ultimate goal is to find the most relevant content on the first search.

Responsiveness is part of the strategy to maintain community vitality. Communities are measured on the ability to respond to questions, even complex ones, quickly. Communities are held to a 48-hour response time; most questions, however, are answered within 24 hours.

Communities are involved in eliminating redundant knowledge repositories, which helps increase the significance of the communities across Fluor. Streamlining databases helps promote the one-stop shop mentality that permeates the organization. As an example, one community was able to eliminate 114 databases to streamline content. Meaningful databases used by small populations are migrated into existing communities. The costs associated with maintaining redundant databases typically exceed the cost to integrate knowledge and properly manage it in a single location. Overall, the aggregation of knowledge is critical and ensures that communities provide the most relevant and valuable knowledge.

Member Engagement   Fluor uses several approaches to support member engagement, including a success story campaign, peer recognition programs, support for subject matter experts, and the inclusion of KM in recruitment and new-hire orientation activities.

Capturing community success stories is key to Fluor's engagement strategy. Success stories are accepted annually and must be related to knowledge sharing. Each year, the organization collects 50 to 80 high-quality stories. Story submissions are reviewed and edited by the core team. A title, value statement, and summary are created for each story to assist with the selection process. Senior-level executives are then asked to review 16 to 20 success stories and select the most relevant and powerful examples. Executives are rotated each year so that a new population is exposed to the powerful impact that communities have on the organization.

Each story is collaborative and demonstrates how communities and knowledge sharing provide value to the organization. Winners of the success story campaign choose a charity to receive a donation on behalf of Fluor. Fluor publicizes why a particular charity is chosen; many times, "the stories are powerful and have a significant impact on sustained community performance," said Tara Keithley, director of communications.

A key component of the core KM team's efforts to collect success stories is the annual "Knowvember" knowledge campaign. This campaign celebrates the expertise and influence in Fluor's communities. Throughout November, community members are asked to submit global success stories, nominate members for outstanding community involvement, and participate in KM workshops around the globe.

Membership engagement is also sustained through peer recognition programs that reward behaviors. Its KM Pacesetter program recognizes community members who actively submit knowledge, act as members, and suggest improvements to the knowledge community. Employees are nominated by their peers and receive a plaque and recognition for community participation. This program is highly successful and helps sustain community engagement.

Engaging subject matter experts is critical to community success. The frequency with which a subject matter expert participates in a community affects the quality and quantity of community content. Experts are chosen by a community. Peer recognition is a powerful engagement agent; it is an honor to be selected by peers. Subject matter experts subscribe to automatic notifications and receive updates when documents require review or feedback. Aligning content and forums with areas of expertise makes it easier to automatically notify subject matter experts when their expertise is needed.

Employees are exposed to Fluor's knowledge-sharing culture during recruitment and new-hire orientation. Specifically, the new-hire orientation materials challenge employees to share knowledge across Fluor's global networks to help the newcomers succeed in the organization. Since career mobility is enhanced by community participation, many employees quickly engage in community activities.

The subject matter expert protégé program is another platform designed to promote early engagement of future experts. The program pairs entry- and mid-level employees with senior-level experts and promotes accelerated learning. Subject matter experts work with employees to create relationships, discuss project technical areas, develop new knowledge, review existing knowledge, and help answer forum questions.

Global Communities   Every community at Fluor is global; this is a requirement. Engaging key geographical locations and worldwide experts is a strategic part of the deployment of the community. The KM core team works with community leaders during deployment and performance reviews to ensure global representation.

Roles

Each community is supported by a community performance team. Each community has a community sponsor and a community leader. The community leader is the highest functional authority for the community. The knowledge manager reports to the community leader and receives support from the KM core team. Knowledge managers are supported by experts and members who serve as knowledge reviewers and forum moderators.

Community Performance Team   Each member of the community performance team has a role, and the expectations associated with this role are clearly communicated. Global excellence leaders (along with community leaders) are responsible for:

- Selection and implementation of best practices
- Selection and support of global reference systems
- Functional people development
- Leadership of their respective knowledge communities
- Development and maintenance of a functional network that crosses business groups

Knowledge Community Leader At Fluor, global network performance is directly linked to active and involved community leadership. On average, community leaders spend 20 percent of their time on functional development. Community leaders are required to:

- Oversee the design, purpose, and strategic direction of a knowledge community
- Implement and execute the community charter
- Monitor community performance
- Identify and develop functional expertise
- Update and maintain global practice, procedures, and templates
- Leverage best practices across offices and business groups
- Serve as a visible role model of desired knowledge-sharing behaviors

As noted, community leaders are the highest authorities in their functional communities, as well as the most visible members. Active engagement for the community is an essential characteristic of a community leader.

The community leader is supported by other key roles in the community. Department managers, regional leaders, knowledge managers, subject matter experts, and moderators provide leadership and vital support. Department managers and regional leaders are expected to participate in network phone calls and provide local contacts for community issues. The knowledge manager oversees organization-wide content and supports leadership with other initiatives as needed and requested. Subject matter experts help with practice and procedure updates and participate in protégé programs. Finally, forum moderators are responsible for forum responsiveness and expert engagement.

Knowledge Managers Each community has a knowledge manager who is responsible for community maintenance and support. Community leadership is not delegated to the knowledge manager; rather, a community knowledge manager supports community activities and facilitates content creation and storage. Knowledge managers are expected to:

- Facilitate, monitor, and support the knowledge processes within the community
- Manage content
- Review and approve (with subject matter expert input) knowledge submissions
- Encourage new content creation
- Initiate cross-community collaboration
- Protect intellectual property
- Manage community projects
- Provide community member recognition
- Participate in knowledge-sharing calls and meetings
- Network with other knowledge managers

Knowledge managers also manage forum moderators and work closely with subject matter experts. The knowledge manager role is an excellent growth opportunity. On average, knowledge managers work in the role for an 18- to 30-month term. Ideal knowledge managers must have two to seven years of experience in the community's function or business and at least two years with Fluor. Managers should also be high-potential employees.

Subject Matter Experts   The subject matter expert is a key member of the community performance team. Subject matter experts are expected to:

- Share expertise through discussion forums
- Update practices and procedures
- Recognize others through the KM Pacesetter program
- Mentor community members
- Promote KM programs and the use of Knowledge OnLine

Subject matter experts are also asked to assist with the development of new knowledge. Filling knowledge gaps, reviewing and approving new knowledge, and maintaining knowledge packets are some of the tasks performed by subject matter experts. Community training is available to help subject matter experts understand their role.

Technology for Communities

Single-point access is part of a larger philosophy of standardization. The ability to provide one-stop shopping is more than a slogan; it's a strategic imperative. Fluor's Knowledge OnLine portal is the home page for every employee and provides access to communities of practice, knowledge-sharing activities, resources, and intellectual property.

Simple and centralized are the guiding principles of KM at Fluor, and the organization's technology solutions support that strategy. Employees log in only once to access all communities in Knowledge OnLine. Teams need to have access to all intellectual capital in the organization; accordingly, a robust technology platform incorporates all resources, including communities.

Fluor's existing technology infrastructure provides features similar to those found in Web 2.0. "We focus our energy on knowledge-sharing behaviors and culture change. Our aim is to connect people to people and the knowledge they need," McQuary said.

Figure A.3 shows Web 2.0 technologies in comparison to KM at Fluor. As shown, whereas social networks are a primary objective of Web 2.0, Fluor's strategy focuses on profiles and networks. Blogging

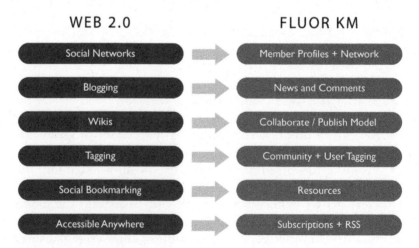

Figure A.3   Web 2.0 and KM at Fluor

is an objective of Web 2.0; Fluor relies on news and comments within Knowledge OnLine.

Cultural Enablers for Sustaining Communities

Fluor has a strong history of knowledge sharing, much of which is attributed to a culture that consistently supports such behaviors. The organization promotes a culture that is based on sharing knowledge across a network of employees. Leaders play an important role in sustaining this culture.

The attitudes and behaviors of senior leaders have a profound impact on the organization as a whole. Fluor's CEO and executives frequently promote Knowledge OnLine and communicate the importance of knowledge sharing in speeches and reports. Even the annual report refers to the importance of knowledge sharing several times.

Training New-hire orientations incorporate training on knowledge-sharing methods and tools. One of the training modules specifically addresses KM and introduces new hires to communities. Community information and assistance is reviewed during the course, and community leaders and experts are identified. A number of courses provide basic KM training and community-specific objectives. Some of Fluor's formal KM training courses are:

- Introduction to Knowledge Management
- Subject Matter Expert KM Workshop
- Forum Moderator Training
- Knowledge Manager Training
- Community Leadership

Subject matter experts receive training on tools, communications, and processes. The training helps them understand the process for updating policies and procedures and walks them through the knowledge approval process.

Communication Each community must complete a performance and communication plan. The plan is reviewed when a community is launched and updated annually.

Community communications are designed to be quick and targeted. For example, the core team prepares a quarterly newsletter targeted to executives across the corporation on KM activities. "We plan for it quarterly; but if there is nothing important to send, we don't do it," Keithley said.

The strategy is to limit spam and irrelevant communications; newsletters and communications focus on major awards or unique activities that capture the attention of executives.

Communities publish newsletters for their membership and receive support from the core team, if needed. Some newsletters, such as *Engineering Quarterly*, are robust and shared across related communities. The newsletter is reshaped to appear more relevant to linked communities and provides hyperlinks to access more information.

The Knowledge OnLine home page is changed every 2.5 days to enhance communication. Internal news or external events are often featured in community home pages.

Participation Recognition The organization's fellows program is one way employees receive recognition for contributions to technical excellence. The program recognizes individuals who obtain the highest level in a technical or functional career track. Fellows and senior fellows are not only the highest ranking experts in the organization; they must obtain outside recognition as well. Fellows are asked to disseminate knowledge through training sessions, seminars, personal contact, and participation in knowledge communities. McQuary said: "You don't become a fellow sitting in your cubicle. If you can't share your knowledge and mentor others, the fellows program is not for you."

Peer recognition is built into the community structure. Every year employees can be nominated for the KM Pacesetter program, which recognizes good knowledge-sharing behaviors. Employees are nominated for the award for actively submitting knowledge, reporting gaps, reviewing new knowledge and forum activity, and community participation. Pacesetters also encourage others by demonstrating knowledge-sharing behaviors and suggesting improvements to the knowledge community. Leading a community or mentoring other employees would also support a nomination for a Pacesetter award.

On average, several hundred KM Pacesetter nominations are made each year. Winners receive a plaque that is given to them by their local office manager during a lunch or special event to honor the recipient. "There is no such thing as too much recognition," said

Keithley. "If someone does something good out there, we want to tell them how much we appreciate their efforts." Overall, the award provides a way for members to receive peer recognition and encourages community engagement.

Measuring Communities of Practice

Fluor's communities are measured on performance and organizational effectiveness. Audits are used to help communities improve. When an audit is conducted, it is shared with community leaders to help determine areas of focus. Audits help determine how communities are organized and identify areas for improvement. Communities are audited in six functional areas to assess performance and effectiveness:

1. Community organization
2. Performance measurement
3. Knowledge community structure
4. Managing knowledge community content
5. Communicating and recognition
6. Encouraging innovation

Each focus area asks a series of questions to identify gaps in organization, structure, content, or innovation. For example, the audit asks questions pertaining to subject matter experts, such as the number of subject matter expert profiles that are up to date and if expectations are clearly communicated. These sections are used during knowledge manager training to help community managers understand how a successful community should function.

A community dashboard is available in the community administration site to provide easy access to performance measures. Managers can quickly access statistics on active members by office, submission history, member activity, or most-often-read knowledge. The dashboard also shows the number of documents that need review or questions that are awaiting replies.

The organization also captures evidence of community value through member testimonials and feedback. Fluor employs a number of individuals who are recognized by outside industries as leading scientists and thought leaders. It is common for these individuals to respond to a new-hire question or inquiry. In one case, a well-known scientist personally replied to a request, which showed the commitment to communities at all levels in the organization. Another story showed how a new employee was able to troubleshoot a problem from the field by leveraging expertise in Knowledge OnLine. Fluor captures these stories to show how communities consistently deliver intangible value to the organization.

Fluor is able to attach a specific cost savings figure to some success stories. For example, in Kuwait, access to design materials, expert responses, and project references led to a recommendation that saved Fluor's client approximately €1 million. Moreover, additional work for another refinery was secured because the client was pleased with the services provided by Fluor team members.

Assessing Community Health   Before a community is deployed, it must develop a community performance and communication plan, which outlines focus areas, performance objectives, and necessary communications. This document is updated throughout the life span of the community. A separate section captures comments on progress. In essence, the document outlines communication strategies and provides access to tools that can help sustain a community.

Community health and performance are tracked and reviewed by the core KM team. A healthy community has both quality and quantity in forums, discussions, and content. Healthy communities also maintain business alignment and achieve stated objectives. Ongoing performance meetings are held to ensure that a community continues to provide business value.

Maintaining Alignment with Business Processes   Fluor's organizational reporting structure ensures that communities align with business processes and objectives. Specifically, the vice president of KM and technology strategy reports to the vice president of project execution services, who reports to the president of operations and the CEO. This structure provides governance to ensure that KM and communities are aligned with the overall business strategy.

Critical Success Factors

At Fluor, critical success factors for sustaining communities focus on people, processes, leadership, culture, and value. A focus on people is paramount to all activities. "It really comes down to an emphasis on people," said Keithley. "You can't lose sight of the fact that communities are really about connecting people."

Employees form the core of Fluor's knowledge-based service strategy. Enthusiastic people, active and involved leadership, and strong people networks are critical to success. It is equally important to define and communicate knowledge-sharing expectations to leaders, knowledge managers, and subject matter experts.

To sustain communities, it is important to make sure that early success stories become daily occurrences. Strong community sponsorship must communicate value on a regular basis and promote community engagement.

To be effective, communities at Fluor must:

- Embed KM into work processes
- Leverage innovations
- Support community leadership transitions
- Embrace KM as part of the culture
- Provide customer value recognition
- Align objectives with business strategy
- Emphasize communications
- Share knowledge across boundaries
- Continually raise performance expectations
- Adjust roles as the company transforms into a knowledge-based organization

At Fluor, communication strategies use storytelling and share progress toward objectives. It is important to share external recognition as well; it often provides internal credibility for community efforts. Sharing knowledge across boundaries also is critical. Organizations should begin with the enterprise in mind and deploy communities globally, and communities should be open to all employees to better enhance their effectiveness.

Finally, knowledge communities cannot succeed without technology platforms to support them. Accordingly, the creation of an organization-wide, single source to connect employees regardless of location or time differences is a critical success factor for sustaining communities.

IBM

IBM provides business insight and IT solutions to help its clients become more efficient and competitive. IBM operates in 170 countries and maintains a work force of 370,000 employees serving the financial services, public, industrial, distribution, small and medium business, and communications sectors. The organization's five major lines of business are global business services, global technology services, systems and technology, software, and global financing.

IBM's Global Business Services (GBS) division, which we focus on in this Appendix, provides professional services and application outsourcing services focused on:

- *Consulting and systems integration.* Consulting services for client relationship management, financial management, human capital management, business strategy and change, and supply chain management.
- *Application management.* Services related to application development, management, maintenance, and support for packaged software, as well as custom and legacy applications.

This division represents approximately 150,000 employees globally, most of whom work at client sites or telecommute. IBM GBS maintains a robust learning and knowledge organization that provides:

- *Knowledge-sharing services.* Community- and practitioner-driven knowledge sharing, a unified learning and knowledge experience, and infrastructure and core enablement.
- *Education services.* Development and delivery of virtual, componentized curriculum.
- *Benchmarking services.* Using an open standards approach to provide self-service capabilities and specific support.

GBS's learning and knowledge organization is focused on promoting a knowledge-sharing culture through effective processes, technical infrastructure, business research services, content management, and communities of practice. And IBM GBS uses its KM strategy as a competitive differentiator—that is, as evidence of being a thought leader in their areas of expertise.

History of KM in IBM GBS

At IBM GBS, KM has progressed through three distinct phases.

In the first phase, KM was decentralized. All KM programs across the organization were designed and owned by separate entities, and business areas were free to create their own repositories, infrastructure, and processes.

In the second phase, KM was centralized to optimize resources, increase efficiency, and minimize costs.

In the third phase, GBS created its learning and knowledge organization to integrate KM processes and tools and simplify the overall process to share knowledge. During its first five years, the learning and knowledge organization was responsible for many elements of the content life cycle, including content harvesting, approvals, and archiving. Also, a team of support personnel was made available to help employees find information and people.

In 2008, the learning and knowledge organization transformed its knowledge-sharing approach, including how it integrates people, processes, and technologies. Previously, the organization had focused its KM services on KnowledgeView, a global asset repository. This intranet portal provided reusable assets to people across GBS. In shifting to a social software–based self-service model, the organization created a new practitioner portal that improves access to content and people by leveraging social computing tools, user involvement, and fluid knowledge in communities.

"We've been on a change agenda," said Bryant Clevenger, global knowledge strategy leader at IBM Global Business Services. "In the past, we had KnowledgeView, which was content-rich and had robust search and navigation capabilities. We've changed our whole approach, though, to a new Web 2.0–based portal and behavior model that leverages user activity while requiring less formal infrastructure support. The whole working structure of our organization is now different. We feel we have greater capabilities, better user enablement, and lower overhead. The core of this new model is the Web 2.0 technologies."

GBS's learning and knowledge organization cites a number of forces that drove GBS toward a new knowledge-sharing model:

- The amount of content being created and consumed is increasing exponentially, making it impossible to formally codify all knowledge.
- It is hard to identify a set group of subject matter experts because the definition of *expert* is contextual.
- The most valuable intellectual capital is often tacit.

- The global nature of business makes it difficult to cultivate personal networks.

Because employees need hard-to-codify information to do their jobs and because people's natural inclination is to exploit their social networks, the learning and knowledge organization decided to design its knowledge-sharing approach around the exchange of tacit knowledge through human networks.

As part of this effort, the organization has redesigned GBS's strategy for expertise location and social networking. Traditionally, the division's expertise location approaches included:

- BluePages, a corporate directory
- Practitioner Support Network, a person-brokered service
- BlueGroups, e-mail, and distribution list management
- Forums with support for formal and informal communities
- Other common means such as telephone and Rolodex

"A lot of people use BluePages to search for people," Clevenger said. "But I don't really think of it as an expertise location system. It contains a wealth of facts, but lacks any contextual information or social networking data. Our practitioner support network also used to provide a service around finding experts. As we have introduced new tools, however, we have been able to adapt the scope of this network to focus on analytical research, while expertise location is provided in a self-service manner through the portal. Our objective is to put new capabilities in front of people so that they don't have to rely on other people to find expertise."

GBS's practitioner portal provides a single point of access to people, content, and knowledge-sharing services. A federated search function integrates multiple repositories and social applications. The portal has a distributed content ownership model that incorporates social computing and automated expertise location. Through the use of Web 2.0 tools, GBS embraces activities such as social bookmarking and tagging. Instead of relying on application-specific functionality, the new model focuses on Web services that feed up through the portal, and the nature of the platform will enable GBS to integrate new capabilities more quickly and easily.

Transforming the Way IBM Works

Bryant Clevenger, lead knowledge sharing strategist, shared with APQC: "It isn't about technology; it is about behaviors. Web 2.0 technologies provide the technology that can now facilitate the behavior and social dynamics that we are trying to achieve—it completely transforms the way we work."

The practitioner portal and its Web services model unlock hidden knowledge and expertise, tap into the power of extended social networks to increase knowledge sharing and collaboration, and optimize the value of content through social networks. For employees, the knowledge-sharing model simplifies the process of locating experts and expertise. As detailed in Figure A.4, the learning and knowledge organization wants to provide social solutions that offer users business value.

The learning and knowledge organization is currently focusing its expertise location approach on data and how they can be

PROFESSIONAL DEVELOPMENT	PRODUCTIVITY
• Increase visibility, recognition, and reputation in organization	• Accelerate time to locate and access expertise
• Foster personal connections and grow their personal networks	• More rapid identification of people who can positively influence business outcome
• Promote continuous learning–knowledge-sharing culture	• Increase opportunities for innovation
	• More expedient knowledge creation and sharing
KNOWLEDGE SHARING	COLLABORATION
• Increase awareness and leverage of expertise in the business as it evolves	• Increase amount of informal and formal cross-department and cross-geo collaboration
• Increase cross-department and cross-geo collaboration	• Visibility of formal and informal communities —information flow and collaboration and health of network
• Accelerate pervasive dissemination of knowledge (codified and tacit)	• Visibility of expertise and faster reciprocal contact due to social network introductions
• Optimize the use of content through social networks	• Increase efficiency and effectiveness of collaboration

Figure A.4   Value Matrix for IBM GBS's New Knowledge-Sharing Model leveraged through analytics. "We don't staff people to serve exclusively as experts," Clevenger said. "The experts are people out on project sites, so we have to tap into that wherever it occurs naturally."

Analytics drive the technology landscape for expertise location and social networking. Automation and federated search functionality reduce the organization's distributive labor model while extending the reach of knowledge held by individual employees and communities of practice.

"Like most consulting organizations, our consultants have utilization targets," Clevenger said. "Formal knowledge-sharing activities are sometimes perceived as detracting from utilization, so we're trying to give our users fast, easy access to content and people so they can be more effective and efficient. As part of our shifting model, we're simplifying and automating the contribution process as much as possible. We expect our new model not to be perceived as a hit to utilization, but instead as a performance-enhancing enablement that is a fundamental part of people's jobs."

Processes and Tools

As an aggregation of several back-end services, the practitioner portal's main purpose is to provide a single point of entry with easy navigation. IBM has a primary corporate intranet site, but the practitioner portal acts as the hub for learning and knowledge activities within GBS. (Other lines of business within IBM have their own portals, although they may share some underlying services.)

The practitioner portal is organized into *portlets,* which are unique sets of services and content derived from many different sources. Within each portlet are tabs to enable searches, expertise location, and business functionality. Many aspects of the portal can be personalized so that users see only the information they need to do their jobs. Personalization can include anything from major applications, networks, and communities to less formal applications such as currency calculators or time zone clocks.

A major feature of the practitioner portal is its federated search, which pulls content from various IBM knowledge asset repositories and other sources into a single search interface. The resources aggregated in federated search include documents, wikis, community libraries, employee profiles, and on-demand training. Users can search these knowledge assets using social tags or their own search strings and then easily refine results.

Although the list of Web services available through the practitioner portal remains fluid, current services include:

- A federated search for content across multiple sources, including asset repositories and wikis
- A SmallBlue/Atlas–enabled search for expertise and social networks
- A service that connects employees to designated experts through the instant messaging functionality embedded in key enterprise applications
- A customizable "My Place" tab where users can add any portlets they desire
- A social bookmarking feature for individuals and teams to store, catalog, and share URL bookmarks
- RSS feeds for Web sites or any new or changed content
- Notifications summarizing specific employees' tagging activities

Several of these Web services are described in detail in the following sections.

SmallBlue/Atlas   One of the Web services provided through the practitioner portal is called SmallBlue (commercially known as *Atlas for Lotus Connections*), which is a statistical expertise and social network inference platform and search engine developed by GBS's learning and knowledge organization in partnership with IBM research and IBM software services for Lotus.

SmallBlue combines data from the IBM internal public domain with statistical data contributed by consenting opt-in users to make inferences about people's expertise in particular areas and generate an organization-wide social network map. The SmallBlue service enables GBS employees to locate knowledgeable colleagues in their social networks, formal and informal communities, and across the organization.

Suggested social paths enable people to reach out and collaborate with colleagues in an expedient manner. SmallBlue also enables employees to view, manage, and optimize their own personal social networks. SmallBlue analyzes numerous data sources (social computing tools, its social network sensor software, and public data) to make deductions about social networks and expertise. The data are aggregated and used to create the inference indexes that power the SmallBlue tools.

As a social network tool, SmallBlue has been designed to respect individual employees' privacy. Users contribute on an opt-in basis, and the system allows participating users to select terms to be excluded from analysis. In addition, the SmallBlue service supports a master list of terms that are not searched or indexed.

The SmallBlue engine is used to power four distinct tools:

1. *SmallBlue Find.* This tool helps employees locate knowledge-able colleagues by identifying people within existing social networks and across the organization who have information on a given search topic.
2. *SmallBlue Reach.* This tool helps employees analyze lists of suggested connections and decide who to contact. The tool presents the social networking path connecting the employee to each potential expert along with formal and informal views of each expert's interests and knowledge.
3. *SmallBlue Net.* This tool helps employees visualize the social networks associated with particular subject areas by displaying social network diagrams for expertise searches, distribution lists, and communities.
4. *SmallBlue Ego.* This tool helps employees understand and capitalize on the value of their personal social networks by creating visualizations of those networks. The visualizations reveal various colleagues' potential social network value by displaying the types of people to whom those colleagues are connected.

When an employee conducts a search using SmallBlue Find, the system displays the top 100 people associated with the search topic (i.e., the 100 people most knowledgeable about the topic according to the inferred data). Users can filter the results to locate experts within their immediate and extended social networks; results can also be refined by parameters such as country and line of business. From the search results, employees can see contact information for each expert as well as the social networking path that connects them to that individual. Clicking on a person's picture in the SmallBlue Find search results automatically opens SmallBlue Reach.

SmallBlue Reach helps employees look through SmallBlue Find search results and identify the best person to approach for information on a particular topic. For each knowledgeable colleague, SmallBlue Reach displays a description of the person's skills; a list of the communities to which that person belongs; and links to the person's contributions to blogs, forms, and social bookmarking tools. This enables users to delve into the details of each connection's expertise and determine who is most likely to have the necessary knowledge.

Once an employee has chosen a colleague to contact, SmallBlue can show the employee how to get an introduction by listing the connections that the employee has in common with the colleague. Employees can even view visualizations of social networks based on community memberships, social tags, expertise, or organizational hierarchy. Using inferred data about extended social networks, the tool displays the social network path to each colleague and related content that the colleague has tagged as recommended.

The SmallBlue/Atlas team is developing the application by leveraging extended social network and expertise data gained through SmallBlue to improve search functionality and content recommendations. For example, the Synergy Search tool will allow an employee to enter a search term and then provide personalized results based on content that the employee's social network has tagged as relevant to that topic.

The SmallBlue/Atlas team also plans to develop additional social content recommendation services. Its SmallBlue Whisper tool will use social networking and social bookmarking to recommend content based on what others within an employee's social network are tagging. This aggregation prevents the need for people to subscribe individually to colleagues' bookmarks.

The IBM social bookmarking service provides users with the ability to store, catalog, and share URL bookmarks. In other words, users can see their own bookmarks plus those of any other users. Tagging is integrated into the federated search and users can filter results by social tags. Data are also used for social network–based content recommendation services and to provide a person-centered view of content. Users are able to view the name of an individual that has tagged a certain site and can even search by person to view what a given person has tagged. A watch list can be created as well to track what an individual tags on a daily basis. Although relatively new, adoption of the tagging service is growing steadily.

A rating system provides users with the ability to identify the best and most reusable content. Using a browser plug-in that pops up on a user's window, individuals can rate a document using a simple 1 to 5 scale. Users can also provide comments on the document, and others can view comments at any time. Ratings are compiled in a central database and are compared to other ratings to produce an average quality rating. Content rates are factored into the search and indexing results, which ultimately serves to highlight the collective wisdom of GBS. As with social tagging, the adoption of rating is new but growing steadily.

IBM GBS has also deployed a simplified contribution form to promote quick and easy contribution of assets. In the past, users were required to complete multiple required fields in order to contribute data. The process was detailed, cumbersome, and time-consuming. In order to promote contributions as part of daily work, there are now three key fields required in order to contribute content. Title, abstract, and attachment are the only fields required for submission. This reduced number of required fields makes contributing simple and fast. The contribution form leverages a streamlined taxonomy, autotagging, and social-bookmarking functionality to simplify and improve search capabilities.

Autotagging of submitted content and federated search content enables a blended approach of user-generated folksonomy (social tagging) with a slimmed-down formal taxonomy. Users do not have to assign any tags; the technology does all the work. Content is automatically analyzed, and a confidence level is attached. Content that has a low confidence rating may need to be manually reviewed. The expectation is that the contribution level will significantly increase because of the simplified process and form.

IBM GBS has also changed how documents are archived. In the past, the process to determine if content needed to be archived was extensive and time consuming. It was mainly a manual process, which involved engaging the original authors of content or subject matter experts to review and edit documents that became dated over time. The reviewers could then stipulate whether content should remain or be archived.

Today, user content and contributions drive the way assets are maintained and archived. Each document is assigned an activity score that is derived from factors such as the number of social tags, net user rating, and number of hits. These data are then transformed into an aggregate activity score over a 12-month period. If for any reason a document does not reach a threshold of activity in a rolling 12-month period, then it is automatically archived. This process relieves users of the unnecessary burden of manually archiving documents.

Wikis are emerging as a popular technology to support collaborative sharing, innovation, and informal learning. Users can search and edit wikis from the central wiki platform, WikiCentral, and although owners can control the structure of and access to a wiki, most wikis are open for anyone to edit. Wikis have a wide range of uses. Some practice areas and business segments uses wikis to serve as community spaces. Other wikis are used to communicate leadership messages, key news, and events or to promote collaboration.

BluePedia is IBM's digital encyclopedia. BluePedia provides a more traditional encyclopedia view; users can find and edit existing articles or create new ones. Social bookmarking enhances the ability to find articles and is built into the system.

The use of blogs is also rapidly expanding in the organization and is used as a collaborative medium that augments wikis and formal asset repositories. Subscriptions, tags, and ratings enhance users' abilities to find and use blog entries. The volume of blog usage is growing steadily. The blogging guidelines reflect the standard code of business guidelines for the organization. In other words, employees are encouraged to share ideas internally and behave in the same professional manner that is reflected in general business conduct. There are no different expectations on behavior internally; however, there are limitations as to what can be shared externally. IBM had 125 external blogs by 2010.

Making Experts Available at a Teachable Moment   In 2005, IBM began working on a way for employees to contact designated experts directly from e-learning or other online applications. The objective was to provide just-in-time access to expertise through an IM application so that neither experts nor those in need of knowledge would have to access a separate system in order to interact. (We would describe this as an approach to ensure questioners can reach out to experts without leaving the flow of their work or training.) This core service is now being leveraged in many applications around the organization, including the practitioner portal.

The service is embedded in more than 200 different applications at IBM, connecting peers and experts by IM or e-mail in the context of parent applications. The participating experts volunteer to answer questions during certain hours in addition to performing their typical, day-to-day responsibilities. Once an expert has answered a particular question by IM, the text from the chat can be incorporated into a FAQ and made available to future knowledge seekers. The tool identifies officially recognized experts who have made themselves available to answer questions on specific topics.

"One of our biggest uses of this system is in our systems and technology group," said Laurie Miller, an expertise program manager in IBM Learning. "A huge number of people are retiring soon, and there is no way to ask all of those people to please write down everything they know. There's also a shortage of young people coming out of college who want to go through core dumps and learn things like C++. So we've tried to figure out a way to make these people who have critical knowledge available, when they can be, to other people with questions."

Organizational and Cultural Issues

IBM's embrace of Web 2.0 technologies has led to a cultural shift at the organization, as well as a shift in focus for GBS's learning and knowledge organization. "We think of ourselves now [as] in a perpetual beta," Clevenger said. "Two years ago, we had a much more traditional software life cycle model, where we would receive many requirements, prioritize them, and deploy those we were able to fund on an annual cycle. We became dissatisfied with that model and the length of time it took from requirement to deployment. Today, we have changed the model so that we consider ourselves more in a perpetual beta, always evolving and improving. Our approach now is that we strive to get capabilities out more quickly and be more flexible to user feedback."

According to Clevenger, Web 2.0 applications allow GBS to meet evolving knowledge-sharing needs more effectively because such technologies make it easier to take risks and experiment. The fluid nature of the practitioner portal enables the organization to quickly launch and test new functionality while improving existing applications and services.

When the portal was launched in 2008, it was tested by pilot projects and focus groups before it was introduced to the wider GBS employee base. Virtual training is available in the form of short, instructional videos and online help documents, but the team believes that using the portal is largely intuitive. "We are leveraging a training model much like YouTube or Facebook, where there is little formal education required," Clevenger said.

A key feature of the Web services available through the practitioner portal is its voluntary nature. For SmallBlue, employees must opt in before certain data about them are used by the system. Employees can opt out of any feature or function and can ask that their information be excluded from any given expertise topic. Similarly, for the more formal expertise location applications, experts must explicitly agree to be included. All the Web services comply with IBM's corporate privacy and data protection policies.

Impact: Indicators and Measures of Success

"Even though this toolset is relatively new, adoption trends are heading in the right direction," Clevenger said. "We had over 100,000 searches in SmallBlue from when it was first launched February to October 2008."

During the first seven months that the IM expertise location service was available, experts from 16 service areas and 23 countries volunteered to participate. More than 4,000 questions were asked, and experts spent almost 60,000 minutes answering those questions. The service has been embedded in 200 internal IBM Web applications, including the practitioner portal, a help desk application, and various communities.

This level of interest in expertise location reflects IBM employees' general embrace of Web 2.0 technology. For instance, several million wiki pages were viewed in the first 10 months of 2008. During that same time, 130,000 blog entries were written by 63,000 employees. Clearly, IBM's workforce is excited about Web 2.0 applications and eager to adopt new social applications. This cultural current bodes well for the future of the organization's expertise location Web services.

Lessons Learned and Future Plans

IBM GBS's learning and knowledge organization cites the following lessons learned from its experience developing and launching social networking and expertise location toolset described in this case study:

- *Engage your organization's legal department and privacy experts early in the process.* It can take a long time to get approval. "The last thing you want to do is invest your time and find out later that you are in violation of the law," Clevenger said.
- *Determine what is indicated by various data sources.* When mining data about employees' knowledge, make sure that you differentiate between expertise and interest. Someone may be interested in a particular topic, but that does not make that person an expert. For this reason, IBM chose not to mine wiki and blog content when making inferences about expertise.
- *Usability and user experience are critical.* "We try not to get in our own corner to develop something," Clevenger said. "We engage users to define the problems we need to solve and validate functionality."
- *Leverage the power of analytics, but take privacy into account.* Web 2.0 technology provides a great opportunity to centralize search services while mining social networking data for valuable content, and organizations should take advantage of that. However, it is important not to impinge on people's privacy.
- *Analytics alone are not enough.* Even when introducing automated solutions, success requires leveraging context and getting people involved.

"The opportunities for leveraging social networking data are huge," Clevenger said. "We've only scratched the surface. We'll cast the net wide and then pull into the portal the capabilities that add the most value."

MITRE

The MITRE Corporation is a nonprofit organization chartered to work in the interest of the American public. The organization provides expertise in systems engineering, IT, operational concepts, and enterprise modernization to address the critical needs of its sponsors, including the U.S. Department of Defense, the Federal Aviation Administration, and the Internal Revenue Service. Acting as an independent adviser, it manages three federally funded research and development centers for those sponsors.

In addition to two principal locations in Bedford, Massachusetts, and McLean, Virginia, MITRE has sites located across the country and around the world. With 6,800 scientists, engineers, and support specialists, MITRE also has a research and development program that explores new technologies to solve sponsors' problems in the near and long term.

MITRE is organized into four primary business units:

1. The Center for Advanced Aviation System Development
2. The Center for Integrated Intelligence Systems
3. The Command and Control Center
4. The Center for Enterprise Modernization

History and Objectives of KM

MITRE's workforce can be described as technically skilled and highly collaborative. It works side by side with its sponsors, often outside MITRE's offices. At any given time, MITRE's workforce is involved in about 1,800 projects.

"It is a challenge to keep track of who is doing what," said Jean Colbert, a lead software systems engineer at MITRE. "It really is incumbent on every person to know who else is working in their space and network with those people to share our collective intelligence."

KM strategy and goals include enabling easier expertise location and a more robust, targeted professional profile. Related goals are anticipating and delivering information and strengthening MITRE's person-to-person knowledge transfer ability.

Governance and Funding

Organized within and funded by MITRE's chief information office, the KM program is situated in a knowledge services and corporate communications division that operates in parallel with the IT function. Two people, in a part-time capacity, lead the KM program and its six distributed knowledge managers. MITRE's knowledge services team manages the end user–facing services of information retrieval and delivery, community and team support, KM collaboration guidance and training, and information navigation.

The Business of Knowledge

Jean Tatalias, director of knowledge services, told APQC: "Everyone at MITRE is considered a knowledge worker. We don't sell software, and we don't compete in the software world. We are in the business of knowledge, and we use our knowledge to help the government improve its operations and capabilities."

All hardware and software components of MITRE's KM strategy are managed by the IT function. Specifically, IT manages the infrastructure components such as Windows technology, intranet, portal applications, SharePoint, team rooms, and network. Both areas are supported by the innovation and planning function, which researches leading-edge technologies and uses pilots to stimulate innovation internally.

All of these functions report to the chief information officer (CIO), who is the champion for knowledge sharing and collaboration. The CEO is also considered a knowledge champion.

Most of MITRE's KM efforts (an estimated 80 percent) are distributed to the businesses. Publishing and stewardship is distributed throughout business functions. Corporate support is limited to a small staff that is responsible for best practices tagging, community support services, and corporate news publishing.

KM services are funded through corporate overhead. Research staff is generally borrowed from library functions and charge their time to project codes. The CIO customer council is a group of individuals that represent business units and reports to the CIO as to what is useful to their respective business units. The program members work with representatives from the business units in a corporate planning, strategy, and championship function to foster knowledge sharing and collaboration. They also support approaches for connecting people and managing knowledge assets for sharing and reuse. Every MITRE project leader can be considered a knowledge steward with KM responsibilities.

Processes and Tools for Knowledge Sharing and Expertise Location

According to Jean Tatalias, director of knowledge services, the organization relies on a set of knowledge-sharing tools instead of a specific KM process. Tatalias said, "We don't use one process; we use a rich set of tools. Some may go away, some may get stronger."

As a result, like many organizations, MITRE struggles to find the balance between the "let a thousand flowers bloom" approach and a more streamlined, process-oriented approach for its Web 2.0 applications. Currently, almost any group or team can pilot a social networking tool; there is no formal gate to approve a pilot. This approach is strategic; the organization finds that this is an effective way to find out what is important to its employee base. However, there is a debate underway on how to impose more governance without reducing enthusiasm and creativity.

MITRE MII   A core KM tool is MITRE's information infrastructure (MII), a corporate intranet and information management system. Implemented in 1994, MII contains a number of knowledge-sharing features and integrates with all of the organization's other expertise location and social networking tools.

Employees gain access to MII through customizable portlets, which include tabs that link to projects and relevant news. On an MII home page, for example, a user will have a menu of links such as *IT services* and *meeting support*. The home page also may list project summaries (e.g., budgets and progress), upcoming events and calendar items, RSS feeds, local weather, favorite links (e.g., MITRE's public server), employee share folders, a time card, and a corporate phone book. A FastJump feature on the portlet allows users to see a tag cloud of the most popular search terms from the last 30 days.

The phone book allows users to search for people, communities, and mail lists. Populated by back-end repositories, including a PeopleSoft database and a Microsoft Outlook calendar, the phone book is Java-based. It includes an availability calendar, core job information, project charges, communities to which the individual belongs, and recently published documents. An "About Me" folder contains résumés. From the phone book, users can request a meeting or add a person to their contact lists.

MII's capabilities are updated continually with major reevaluations every three to five years.

MITREpedia   MITREpedia is an internal wiki for collecting knowledge about MITRE's projects, customers, organizations, technology, and staff. Launched in 2005, the wiki can be used by anyone at MITRE to share and update knowledge about all things relating to the organization. MITREpedia employs an easy-to-use interface, enabling almost 900 unique users across the different centers to share their knowledge. In a typical month, MITREpedia averages more than 25,000 total visits.

As its name suggests, MITREpedia was set up to mirror Wikipedia so that users would be familiar with the concept and functionality. The tool allows tacit knowledge and expertise to be captured from a grassroots perspective. Considered an experimental space for refining ideas, it is used as a quick, easily accessible source of information and as a supplementary cross-reference to communities and projects.

MITREpedia's taxonomy has a loose structure that helps the tool act as a catch-all for MITRE's tacit knowledge. It can run on any operating system, with minimal set-up required and minimal maintenance needed.

ProjectPages Online   ProjectPages Online is a prototype Web-centric project Rolodex that promotes knowledge sharing across the MITRE community, especially with regard to the organization's technical work program. It does so by capturing an engineering snapshot of all of MITRE's technical projects and facilitating knowledge transfer and expertise location among technical staff. By acting as a central source from which to retrieve technical project information, ProjectPages Online promotes transparency across work programs, establishes enduring project histories, and reveals patterns and opportunities for project managers.

"Right now, there's a wealth of information about projects in distributed repositories," said Colbert. "This is a simplified, aggregated look at the technical details. There is a page for each of MITRE's 1,800 current projects. With this, we're starting to move from a document-centric approach to a Web-centric approach."

On a project page in ProjectPages Online, users can find a description of the project, tags, goals, activities, impacts, a list of external partners involved in the project, links to the project's SharePoint community and related MITREpedia articles, and other details such as the size of the project, stakeholders, key milestones, and project staff.

Blogs MITRE uses blogs for self-publishing, disseminating knowledge, and sharing informal information. In 2003, the organization initiated a pilot program titled "Blogs @ MITRE" that provides support for individual and project-based blogs. MITRE also introduced executive blogs in 2008 to encourage candid conversation about MITRE strategies, goals, and plans; this initiative includes blogs by the chief information office and the office of the chief engineer.

Any MITRE employee can access the blogs, which operate on a flexible framework that requires only minor maintenance. The integrated infrastructure includes an Oracle database, ColdFusion Middleware, and Java when needed. All blog content is searchable by MII enterprise search.

Community Share Community Share is MITRE's implementation of Microsoft SharePoint. SharePoint is a collaboration platform that provides a common Web space for managing documents; posting events and announcements; and tracking action items, meeting decisions, and agenda items. Through a central portal, Community Share acts as MITRE's central knowledge repository for all project information.

"It keeps information together and helps us log documents from a project management life cycle perspective," said Michele Smith, SharePoint team lead and service manager at MITRE. Community Share's formal objectives are to:

- Provide a corporate-supported collaboration tool for people to post project-related information
- Educate community leaders on best practices and responsibilities for information sharing
- Encourage consistency in storing valuable content
- Make information about a team or community accessible

Community Share has a decentralized ownership model, with anyone able to request the creation of a project site by filling out an online form. The sites are supported by 10.2 FTEs, including application developers, support liaisons, and a service or project manager. The Community Share team creates and customizes each site, but the community owner is responsible for configuring the site, keeping information up to date, and reminding project team members to use the site. Any project member can add an event or announcement and share or check out documents. If a site is inactive for 90 days, then the Community Share team retires it.

Because MITRE recognizes that online communities are organic, it does not require Community Share's structure to reflect organizational charts or lists of official projects. Each Community Share site has extensive metadata that supports the system's search function, but individual documents stored in Community Share do not have their own metadata. This simplifies the document publication process for end users, although some individual document-retrieval search functionality is sacrificed.

MII Search   Moogle, or MITRE Google, acts as the glue for all of MITRE's knowledge-sharing tools and repositories. In use since 2002, Moogle acts as an enterprise search system for the organization's more than 2.2 million URLs, a core expertise finder and e-mail list searcher, and a source for locating technical exchange meetings. In other words, one search box allows users to retrieve information about people, organizations, projects, social bookmarks, technical issues, and events.

A small team of corporate search-service resources support Moogle, with the production system based on GSA 5005 server. The search functionality indexes:

- 400,000 URLs from the Community Share (SharePoint) document libraries
- 1.4 million URLs from MITRE's Web-enabled file system and distributed Web servers
- 450,000 URLs from e-mail list messages, database crawls, and XML feeds

Search results include tab options, "best bets" (from the MITRE FastJump system), and Google's Onebox feature, which matches people, organizations, relevancy-ranked search results, and technical exchange meeting events.

The Moogle expertise finder function helps new employees; tenured employees who are grappling with new assignments; and increasingly, employees placed in interdisciplinary project teams. A user can start with a topic in a specific search interface and move through applications or repositories (such as community share information). A user can also find a person or group or pose a question directly to members of an e-mail list. Expertise finder search results include source options, e-mail contact options, display options (i.e., *normal view, expand all, unattributed results, search details,* and *organizations*), listings of people with job titles and links to the phone book, and content evidence (with title, links to object and repository, keywords in context, and object date).

The results returned by the e-mail list message search function look like typical Google results. The search function does not mine individuals' inboxes but instead indexes from a shared environment of MITRE listserv e-mail messages.

MITRE tracks the value of Moogle through user surveys, help-desk feedback, and metrics such as queries per month. Based on this input, the organization is looking for better ways to drill down within its expertise finder function and may integrate expertise location with the staff social networking profiles it is developing. Currently, although people use Moogle to find information about employees' backgrounds, the tool is not used to staff projects. To fill this gap, MITRE is developing a staff planning resource assignment tool that will be integrated with Moogle.

Onomi Onomi is MITRE's social tagging and bookmarking tool, funded by corporate IT and integrated with Moogle. This tool allows employees to bookmark resources, tag those resources with metadata and comments, and share bookmarks with other employees. This helps MITRE employees share resources internally, explore topics, discover new communities, find experts, and enhance the value of the organization's other knowledge-sharing tools.

"We have a lot of teams that have to come together quickly to work on diverse projects and domains," said Laurie Damianos, a lead artificial intelligence engineer at MITRE. "So we need to provide ways to share information very quickly. Social bookmarking complements many of our other social networking techniques. We found that a lot of people were already using these tools on the Internet."

As a complement to MITRE's other knowledge-sharing tools, Onomi allows users to share both internal and external resources, thus increasing the number of access points to content. The tool hyperlinks content and enables users to e-mail bookmarks or simply push a bookmark into a public space (i.e., it does not index private bookmarks). Users can retrieve tags and bookmarks through Moogle using parameters such as topic, user, MITRE center, tag, file type, or description. They can also see who is interested in the same topics—thanks to integration with MII's phone book—and receive RSS feeds for every feature (e.g., what a particular organization is posting and bookmarks by topic). Onomi also contains corporate-stewarded collections such as case studies and digital libraries.

The value of Onomi is enhanced by its built-in content life cycle report. For example, the tool scans for broken links and removes them from public view, notifies authors of broken links, and creates temporary accounts so that users can access the bookmarks of employees who have recently left the organization.

MITRE has tracked how Onomi expands knowledge stewardship responsibilities across the workforce. It has found that employees use the tool not only for business resources but also for external Web sites. In addition to supporting individuals, the tool helps teams, subject area social networks, and virtual communities. Fourteen percent of users contribute tags or bookmarks, with that percentage continuing to rise. The tool has 14,000 unique tags and 20,000 bookmarks, 83 percent of which are external bookmarks. This is important in that MITRE employees have no other forum through which to share external resources.

"Onomi allows people to point to information anywhere, so it acts like a virtual repository," Damianos said. "We've seen project teams take a specific tag and use it to mark all of their project-specific resources. Some of the project leaders say this is a great way to find out what their project members are working on or where other team members have put certain things."

TWITRE   TWITRE is a microblogging tool that mirrors Twitter to facilitate social networking and expertise location. MITRE's enterprise architecture planning and innovation function developed TWITRE as a solution for common business problems such as skills finding, staff location awareness, and availability. The tool is a mashup built on commercial social networking tools and is geared to foster knowledge exchange across MITRE's campuses.

From conception to pilot stage, this tool was developed solely by interns. In 2008, MITRE tasked three interns with determining how their generation's most popular tools could be applied to real business problems, such as finding expertise and enhancing collaboration. MITRE also hoped to gain insight into managing business and public personas. The interns observed that MITRE administrative assistants play a key role in people finding one another and knowing the availability of employees to work on projects. These assistants gather expertise and status information from staff members, send daily e-mail updates, and handle phone inquiries. The interns also found this system to be time-consuming, labor-intensive, supported by second-hand information, and dependent on a single point of contact. In response, the interns developed a self-service tool through which employees can broadcast their areas of interest and expertise, locations, and availability: TWITRE.

MITRE employees use TWITRE to post meetings on their calendars and use Microsoft Office's presence indicators to communicate availability. TWITRE's microblogging capabilities allow employees to sidestep the drawbacks of traditional calendars, such as being too focused on meetings, sharing too much or too little information, and not being up to date. TWITRE instead provides a desktop view of each contact's location and availability, an alert system by keywords, a phone-based expertise locator for people outside the MITRE firewall, and touch-screens in common areas. The information is populated by employees' inputs, Twitter feeds, and MITRE's time-reporting system.

During the first three months of the pilot, the tool proved popular even among users who did not previously microblog. The tool strengthened existing connections and fostered new ones. In addition, the public touch-screen became a popular space for socializing.

OneCommunity OneCommunity is a social networking tool for intelligence community professionals that automatically collects information about participants and provides contact recommendations. MITRE intends for OneCommunity to be an integrated set of tools that will direct analysts to others with knowledge that may help them in their work across agencies such as the U.S. armed forces, the U.S.

Defense Intelligence Agency, the Central Intelligence Agency, the Office of the Director of National Intelligence, and the National Geospatial-Intelligence Agency.

This tool is different from MITRE's other expertise locator systems in that users do not need to input keywords to find people. Instead, OneCommunity automatically generates profiles based on online user data and tracking plug-ins (see Figure A.5).

OneCommunity recommends contacts for users by pulling data from multiple sources and then analyzing that data using similarity metrics. Users may enter keywords (or tags from Onomi) that become a searchable part of their skill bases. They may also view heat maps that indicate areas of interest.

OneCommunity's sister research project, MITREVerse, is an MII prototype of the same tool. Both projects are integrated with other MITRE knowledge-sharing tools and built on an open source platform that can easily incorporate new functionality. MITREVerse allows individuals to control who has access to aspects of their profiles and has a separate network for classified information.

MITRE carries out a heuristic usability evaluation to determine the system's usability. It also collects quantitative measures and conducts interviews to gauge user acceptance. To determine whether recommendations are useful and accurate, the organization looks at click-through rates and creates focused experiments to compare system ratings to user judgments. It also analyzes whether the tool

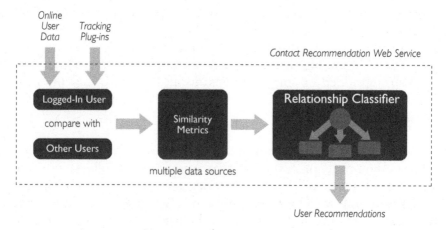

Figure A.5   OneCommunity Process Steps at MITRE

could bolster collaboration by conducting surveys and interviews as well as measuring the number of co-authored products, the size of networks, and participation in online discussions.

Based on these evaluations, MITRE may integrate OneCommunity with external tools, improve its usability, and expand contact recommendations through additional data sources.

Practices for Promoting Engagement and Use

MITRE has conducted a number of campaigns over the years to promote its knowledge-sharing tools. A campaign called Collaborative IQ in 2004 and 2005 promoted—through MII, meetings with managers, desktop reminder cards, and news center stories—sharing, finding, protecting, and stewarding information. In 2008, the communications campaign focused on information protection in an increasingly complex knowledge sharing environment. Also in 2008, MITRE began an information management campaign titled "Seven Essential Steps for MITRE Information Management," which provides guidance to employees on how to manage information. The steps are as follows:

1. Keep project files in Community Share.
2. Share as broadly as possible and protect information according to policy, contractual requirements, and licensing agreements.
3. Use best practices to organize Community Share information.
4. Go beyond simple searches.
5. Manage project and team communication with a tool that works across your team, program, and management needs.
6. Leverage people connections.
7. Customize MII to meet your information needs.

In addition to organization-wide communication campaigns, MITRE bolsters knowledge-sharing tool adoption rates through training. Its fast-forward team is tasked with training employees on any new technology. The team offers webinars, online tutorials, and lunchtime classes. The development team for each MITRE knowledge-sharing tool works with this team to develop training collaboration.

All new hires attend a four-hour orientation that includes an introduction to the MII. Employees are given an overview of the MII and shown how to use the system. The KM function also partners with HR groups and business partners to find out what tools need additional training and development within the MII. Employees can also attend training that introduces new methods and tools. Even employees that have been with the organization for more than 20 years have attended training meetings, simply because technology continues to evolve and the MII is constantly changing.

Organizational and Cultural Issues

As demonstrated by MITRE's numerous and, in some cases, overlapping knowledge-sharing tools, the organization has what Tatalias describes as "a high tolerance for diversity." She said: "This is an expert culture. People want to be recognized for what they know and contribute. Putting your work out there is a way to get recognized. It's innate in our culture."

Beyond this training and support, new technology adoption at MITRE is largely an organic process, with employees free to use whichever tools they deem useful. However, the organization is focused on capturing and applying lessons learned from the deployment of its knowledge-sharing tools. These are often change management and cultural issues.

Challenges and Lessons Learned MITRE has found a number of challenges in deploying social networking and expertise location tools:

- There are human and trust barriers, technological barriers, temporal and geophysical barriers, and security barriers.
- Choosing electronic project files, organizing content, and determining hierarchies and permissions are complex tasks.
- The nature of MITRE's work creates tensions between sharing and securing content.
- It can be a challenge to position the numerous knowledge-sharing tools within MII.
- Users want to customize tools, which can impede supportability.
- Personal metadata quality can vary.

- Not all users are motivated to maintain résumés and profiles online.

In response to these challenges, the organization leverages a number of lessons learned and guidelines:

- By aggregating content, Moogle is the glue that connects the organization's knowledge repositories and collections.
- Employees can be relied on to use tools in a professional manner.
- Nonvalidated expertise can be identified as user-authored or owned content.
- Central infrastructure management and reporting can quickly identify and address issues and manage growth.
- Users adopt tools that suit their work habits. If it works, it works.
- Metadata quality is best when derived or when content collections are stewarded for quality control. It is worst when guidelines are poorly or inconsistently applied.
- MITRE's sponsors are open to tools that will help them collaborate more effectively with MITRE. However, success using new tools may require significant cultural change at sponsor organizations.
- Championship in business units helps guide adoption and tailor knowledge-sharing tools to the needs of different work practices and styles.
- With many knowledge-sharing tools (such as Community Share) not being intuitive, training is key. Create an active training and support program to help users overcome technology hurdles.
- Provide incentives for employees to share information online.
- To overcome trust barriers, offer users opportunities to post personal information and vouch for contacts. And support fine-grained access control for all information.
- Educate users and build buy-in over time. For example, MITRE gained support for Onomi through demonstrations, bookmarks, e-mail announcements, and MII banners.
- Keep tools simple by using existing infrastructures and user-focused interfaces.

- Maintain the right balance of interest and brevity when developing content that will be pushed to users.
- Limit formal data release processes that require a manager's approval to areas where absolutely necessary (e.g., the corporate policies and procedures).
- Develop strategic partnerships with other support organizations to make the best use of new technology.
- Involve technical and business stakeholders in new technology rollouts.
- Secure active and engaged content owners and contributors, such as for Community Share and MITREpedia.
- Automatically update data from open MITRE sources, but be sensitive to the need for privacy in employees' personal communications (such as e-mail).
- Make technology transparent to the user. For example, TWITRE was developed in a manner so that some users are not even aware they are microblogging.
- Pull people in with useful content, even if not work-related, such as weather and traffic reports.
- Target public stewards and librarians in the early stages in order to achieve a critical mass.
- Try to make things easy for users; for example, allow them to automatically import bookmarks from a browser into Onomi.
- Develop applications and repositories that can evolve, be reused, and be added to.
- Use open standards to build in data portability and interoperability as much as possible. Work with existing KM and enterprise 2.0 tools.
- For new technologies, start simple and let the customer create requirements. Then allow the technologies to grow little by little.

With the introduction of social networking and expertise location tools, MITRE has seen a paradigm shift regarding the accessibility of information. Employees are more comfortable with unstructured data, but they want access to advanced search techniques optimized to make sense of that data. Many of the organization's analysts are still not strong users of public social networking tools, but these individuals are starting to believe such tools could add value. Although the most popular communication tools are still chat, e-mail, and telephone, employees want access to professional and personal information about one another.

The adoption of social networking tools at MITRE is propelled by a culture in which individuals want to be known for their contributions and expertise. Knowledge sharing is recognized through a formal reward and recognition program that include an annual President's Award. In addition, the organization's KM and innovation goals are diligently reinforced through corporate goals and leadership directives. Ultimately, the adoption and success of these tools relies on their ability to help employees do their jobs. The tools must be proven to make employees more effective and increase value for MITRE's sponsors.

Impact: Indicators and Measures of Success

MITRE has periodically assessed its overall KM program since 1997. It also measures the use of tools and methods and collects feedback. The organization has a customized approach to determine whether specific tools foster collaboration. For example, to evaluate the OneCommunity tool, it tracks the number of new contacts established and any increase in cross-organizational trust.

The organization administered an employee survey that asked:

- What is the perception of knowledge sharing at MITRE?
- What is the value (i.e., the outcome to the customer) of knowledge sharing at MITRE?
- What KM enablers or activities are in place to support knowledge transfer?
- What are the barriers to knowledge transfer?

The survey found that, although employees tend to prefer Moogle, community share, and an older file-sharing tool, most appreciate the range of the tools available.

Additional Information

The following APQC resources provide additional information on the profiled organizations:

- *Advances in Expertise Location and Social Networking—IBM Global Business Services*

(Continued)

- *Advances in Expertise Location and Social Networking—MITRE Corporation*
- *Retaining Today's Knowledge for Tomorrow's Workforce—Fluor*
- *Sustaining Effective Communities of Practice—ConocoPhillips*
- *Sustaining Effective Communities of Practice—Fluor*
- *Web 2.0 for Knowledge Management—IBM Global Business Services*
- *Web 2.0 for Knowledge Management—MITRE Corporation*

These resources—along with APQC's custom advisory services and more than 1,000 articles focused on KM—are available at www.apqc.org and through this book's Web site at www.newedgeinknowledge.com.

References

Bernoff, Josh, and Charlene Li. 2008. *Groundswell: Winning in a World Transformed by Social Technologies.* Boston: Harvard Business School Press.

CIA. 2009a. "Intellipedia Gurus Win 2009 Homeland Security Medal." Retrieved October 8. https://www.cia.gov/news-information/featured-story-archive/intellipedia-homeland-security-medal.html.

CIA. 2009b. *The World Factbook 2009.* Washington, DC: Central Intelligence Agency. https://www.cia.gov/library/publications/the-world-factbook/fields/2151.html?countryName=&countryCode=xx&regionCode=%B5?countryCode=xx#xx.

DailyFinance. "Best Buy Inc. Company Description." Retrieved July 2, 2010. www.dailyfinance.com/company/best-buy-incorporated/bby/nys/company-description.

Encarta World English Dictionary Online, s.v. "Teachable Moment." Accessed October 29, 2010. http://encarta.msn.com/dictionary_561539567/teachable_moment.html.

Entner, Roger. 2010. "Smartphones to Overtake Feature Phones in U.S. by 2011." *Nielsenwire,* March 26. http://blog.nielsen.com/nielsenwire/consumer/smartphones-to-overtake-feature-phones-in-u-s-by-2011.

Friedlander, Joan. 2010. "Email Interruptions May Lower IQ." *Evan Carmichael.* Retrieved July 2. www.evancarmichael.com/Productivity/3227/Email-Interruptions-May-Lower-IQ.html.

Gaudin, Sharon. 2010. "Twitter Now has 75M Users; Most Asleep at the Mouse." *Computerworld,* January 26. www.computerworld.com/s/article/9148878/Twitter_now_has_75M_users_most_asleep_at_the_mouse.

Giles, Martin. 2010. "A World of Connections: A Special Report on Social Networking." *The Economist,* January 30. www.economist.com/specialreports/specialreportslist.cfm?category=455022.

Grayson, C. Jackson, and Carla O'Dell. 1998. *If Only We Knew What We Know: Transfer of Internal Knowledge and Best Practice.* New York: Free Press.

Hansen, Morten T. 2009. *Collaboration: How Leaders Avoid the Traps, Create Unity and Reap Big Results.* Boston: Harvard Business School Press.

Idinopulos, Michael. 2007. "In-the-Flow and Above-the-Flow." *Transparent Office*, December 26. http://michaeli.typepad.com/my_weblog/2007/12/in-the-flow-and.html.

Li, Charlene, Chris Charron, and Jaap Favier. 2006. *Social Computing: How Networks Erode Institutional Power, and What to Do About It.* Cambridge, MA: Forrester.

Lohr, Steve. 2007. "Slow Down, Brave Multitasker, and Don't Read This in Traffic." *New York Times*, March 25. www.nytimes.com/2007/03/25/business/25multi.html?_r=4&adxnnl=1&pagewanted=all&adxnnlx=1248001246-NdyHv9c/WRNTpPJ58Tb/2A.

Miniwatts Marketing Group. 2009. "Internet World Stats." December 31. www.internetworldstats.com/stats.htm.

Moore, Robert J. 2010. "New Data on Twitter's Users and Engagement." *RJMetrics*, January 26. http://themetricsystem.rjmetrics.com/2010/01/26/new-data-on-twitters-users-and-engagement/.

Nass, Clifford. 2010. "Video Interview." *Digital Nation: Life on the Virtual Frontier*, February 2. www.pbs.org/wgbh/pages/frontline/digitalnation/interviews/nass.html.

Nonaka, Ikujiro, and Hirotaka Takeuchi. 1995. *The Knowledge-Creating Company: How Japanese Companies Create the Dynamics of Innovation.* New York: Oxford University Press.

Pattison, Kermit. 2008. "Worker, Interrupted: The Cost of Task Switching." *Fast Company*, July 28. www.fastcompany.com/articles/2008/07/interview-gloria-mark.html.

PricewaterhouseCoopers. 2007. "Managing Tomorrow's People." www.pwc.com/gx/en/managing-tomorrows-people/future-of-work/pdf/mtp-millennials-at-work.pdf.

Rao, Leena. 2010. "LinkedIn Tops 70 Million Users." *TechCrunch*, June 20. http://techcrunch.com/2010/06/20/linkedin-tops-70-million-users-includes-over-one-million-company-profiles/.

Shirky, Clay. 2010. "Does the Internet Make You Smarter?" *Wall Street Journal*, June 4. http://online.wsj.com/article/SB10001424052748704025304575284973472694334.html.

Surowiecki, James. 2005. *The Wisdom of Crowds: Why the Many Are Smarter Than the Few and How Collective Wisdom Shapes Business, Economies, Societies and Nations.* New York: Anchor.

About the Authors

Dr. Carla O'Dell is president of APQC and is considered one of the world's leading experts in knowledge management.

She wrote with APQC Chairman C. Jackson Grayson *If Only We Knew What We Know: The Transfer of Internal Knowledge and Best Practice* (Free Press 1998), a bestseller that put KM on the map as a practical management discipline. She is also co-author with Grayson of *American Business: A Two Minute Warning* (Free Press 1988) and wrote *The Executive's Role in Knowledge Management* (APQC 2004). She writes frequently for leading journals and magazines and is consistently among the highest-rated speakers at conferences.

The author of more than 18 major best-practice research reports in KM, O'Dell has a unique perspective on what works and what doesn't, what's hype and what's solid. Staying on the leading edge of KM is easy for O'Dell because APQC's members include the best KM professionals and organizations in the world. APQC has conducted 25 consortium studies in KM, with more than 500 participating organizations, and produced the largest body of actionable best practices available in designing, implementing, and measuring KM.

O'Dell began her professional career with the Ford Foundation and the American Center for Quality of Work Life. In the early 1970s, she worked with companies that were just beginning to experiment with new forms of work and new ways to manage people. In 1983, O'Dell served as chairperson of the Rewards Conference of the White House Conference on Productivity. In 1987, she designed and led for APQC the largest national study ever conducted on innovative reward systems, which still serves as the benchmark study in the field.

O'Dell has a bachelor's degree from Stanford University, a master's degree from the University of Oregon, and a doctorate in organizational psychology from the University of Houston.

Cindy Hubert is the executive director of APQC's Advisory Services, which provides individualized and collaborative approaches to solve business problems and address strategic needs.

Over the past 15 years, Hubert and her team have worked with more than 350 organizations to provide assessments, strategy development, project management, transfer of best practice design and implementation, and metric and best practices research engagements using APQC's KM methodologies. She recently led the development of APQC's Levels of Knowledge Management Maturity and KM Capability Assessment Tool, which is used by organizations around the world to guide, develop, and execute their KM strategies and approaches.

Hubert has co-authored with O'Dell a number of KM publications, including APQC's KM Passport to Success Series. She writes frequently for leading journals and magazines and speaks at conferences worldwide.

Hubert has worked with a variety of industries, including oil and gas, manufacturing, pharmaceutical, government and military, retail, nonprofit, and consumer products. Her background includes developing KM strategies, approaches, and supporting measurement systems and integrating with process management and performance improvement initiatives; process redesign; quality programs; and large-scale change efforts supported by training programs, communication strategies, measurement, and competency models. Before being named executive director of custom solutions, Hubert served as the director of KM and learning.

Hubert has also served as an instructor at Rice University's Executive Education Graduate School of Management. A graduate of the University of Texas at Austin, Hubert received a bachelor's degree in business administration and marketing.

About APQC

Since 1977, APQC has been focused on providing organizations with the information they need to work smarter, faster, and with confidence. As one of the world's leading proponents of process and performance improvement, APQC helps organizations around the world improve productivity and quality by:

- Discovering effective methods of improvement
- Broadly disseminating findings
- Connecting employees with one another and with the knowledge they need to improve

APQC is the leading source for best practices and performance benchmarks. With one of the world's largest databases—based on more than 8,500 benchmarking and best-practice studies and growing—APQC members have access to data they can't get anywhere else.

Since bringing the first groundbreaking research on KM to the marketplace in 1990, APQC has continuously refined and standardized reliable frameworks, methodologies, and maturity models for leading organizations around the world. Built on best practices that include an interactive, robust community of KM professionals, APQC is the preeminent source for KM data, knowledge, and expertise.

Unless otherwise attributed, all examples included in this book are from benchmarking studies, presentations, interviews, and research efforts copyrighted by APQC. Visit www.newedgeinknowledge.com to review source materials, and visit www.apqc.org to learn more about APQC.

Index